To Craft Democracies

To Craft Democracies

An Essay
on Democratic Transitions

Giuseppe Di Palma

UNIVERSITY OF CALIFORNIA PRESS

BERKELEY LOS ANGELES OXFORD

University of California Press
Berkeley and Los Angeles, California

University of California Press, Ltd.
Oxford, England

Library of Congress Cataloging-in-Publication Data

Di Palma, Giuseppe.
  To craft democracies : an essay on democratic transitions /
Giuseppe Di Palma.
    p. cm.
  Includes bibliographical references and index.
  ISBN 0-520-07213-8 (alk. paper).—ISBN 0-520-07214-6 (pbk. :
alk. paper)
  1. Democracy. 2. World politics—1945–   I. Title.
JC423.D54 1990
321.8—dc20   90-37202
                                                 CIP

Printed in the United States of America
9 8 7 6 5 4 3 2 1

alle mi' donne
y
a Juan Linz

With a few exceptions, the limits of democratic development in the world may well have been reached.

Samuel Huntington

We must think of the possible rather than the probable.

Albert Hirschman

For what each individual wills is obstructed by everyone else, and what emerges is something that no one willed.

Friedrich Engels

Democratic survival and breakdown [are] a question of political crafting.

Juan Linz and Alfred Stepan

Contents

Acknowledgments

This essay was completed in September of 1989, a few weeks before the events of Hungary, East Germany, Bulgaria, Czechoslovakia, and Romania. Therefore, references to Eastern Europe rely more largely on the case of Poland and the Soviet Union. But the events do not alter that part of the analysis that deals with Eastern Europe, nor its significance for the general thrust of the essay. On the contrary, they confirm it. Thus I have chosen not to update the essay. Let the reader be the judge. (For an update, see my "Democratic Transitions: Puzzles and Surprises from West to East," paper presented at the Conference of Europeanists, Washington, D.C., March 1990. It deals with the rapidity and radicalness of Communist crises and with the central role played by civil society.)

I wish to thank my Berkeley colleagues Jack Citrin and George Breslauer for their criticisms and for sharing with me their expertise. Similarly, I wish to thank Joseph La-Palombara, from Yale University, and Gianfranco Poggi, from the University of Virginia. My very old friendship with them made their criticisms the more bearable, and the more productive. LaPalombara in particular should take credit for giving the title of the essay greater punch by inviting me to stay away from gerunds.

Financial assistance by the Institute of International Studies at Berkeley made writing more comfortable.

The essay is dedicated "to my women," which is meant to refer to my wife, Francine, and my daughter, Vittoria, who assisted at the creation in a friendly and supportive spirit. It is also dedicated to my colleague and friend Juan Linz, whose scholarship and humanity have been a constant and great example. Gentleman that he is, Juan Linz will not object, I'm confident, to taking second billing in the dedication.

Berkeley, January 7, 1990

CHAPTER I

Rethinking Some Hard Facts

Far be it from me to advocate a new social science ortho-
doxy. Yet there is a rekindled public and scholarly interest
in the prospects for democracy in countries where democracy does not now exist. That attention and the renewed
theoretical optimism among a number of scholars deserve a
fair hearing. This essay has been written in defense of that
optimism.

On some grounds the optimism may not seem warranted,
and the skeptics may have a field day. If optimism were based
on democracy's recent record of victories, we should take
note that the record is at least mixed. Since the middle of
the 1970s a number of surprisingly promising transitions to
democracy have occurred. All these transitions were from
right-wing authoritarian regimes—as conventionally understood. All were in southern Europe (Greece, Portugal, Spain)
or South America (Argentina, Brazil). Reacting to those events,
several students of the two areas have eagerly turned their
attention to "democratic transitions." [1]

Yet other transitions—in South America, the Mediterranean, and elsewhere—have been less than promising or inspiring. In South America (Peru, Ecuador, Paraguay, Uruguay, Bolivia), the Mediterranean (Turkey), Central America (El Salvador, Guatemala, Santo Domingo), and Asia (the Philippines, South Korea) the final outcomes of recent democratizing efforts are either uninspiring or difficult to call. Also, expectations that democratization would create regional demonstration effects, carrying along other authoritarian regimes, have so far remained unfulfilled. In South America the Chilean dictatorship has put up a long if apparently losing rearguard action against democratic intrusions. In Central America democracy, reaction, and revolution mix freely and explosively. Prospects look just as unpromising among Marxist or Socialist regimes—despite considerable internal variation (from East European people's democracies to self-styled Marxist regimes in Central America and Africa). Recent momentous developments in Communist Europe promise radical changes, but are we willing to bet on democracy in the short run? Poland and Hungary offer reasons for hope, but regional demonstration effects are still unclear. For all its economic liberalization, China, a continent by itself, seems to be taking steps toward what students of Latin American development call "bureaucratic authoritarianism." And as to Africa as a whole, the prospects we can extrapolate from the postcolonial record seem just as bleak.

Finally, trends toward democratization must be balanced against their counterparts. In Latin America, for example, stable regime types have been rare. Rather, there has been a seesaw between regimes. In general, the 1970s and 1980s have not yet produced that dramatic leap in democratization that followed both world wars. In general, even by the most generous definition of democracy, the proportion of democracies among independent nations is no greater today than it was after World War I.[2]

In sum, the hard facts of trends and numbers do not speak in favor of democracy. And there is another apparent hard fact, closely connected with trends and numbers. The greater the pool of independent nations and the more we move away from the core of long-established Western-style democracies, the more the nations facing democratization fall short of qualities classically associated with Western democracy. Such qualities have been investigated extensively by many influential scholars, mainly in the 1950s and 1960s, and fall into three categories: (1) economic prosperity and equality; (2) a modern and diversified social structure in which nondependent middle classes occupy center stage; and (3) a national culture that, by tolerating diversity and preferring accommodation, is already implicitly democratic. Nations facing democratization without these three characteristics face yet another impediment: democratic transitions are now tending to take place in a climate of mobilization and impatience, if not of outright violence. The benefits of gradualism and accommodation, which have marked the Western experience, would thus be lost.

These are the hard facts weighing on the future of democracy. Indeed, they have led Samuel Huntington to question recent theoretical optimism. He concludes that "with a few exceptions, the limits of democratic development in the world may well have been reached."[3] Is the tail of theoretical optimism trying pointlessly to wag the dog of hard facts? Is the optimism largely a fad—another example of the social scientist who obliges tenuous events?

The hard facts (albeit not all of them) miss some points; in fact, they miss *the* point. Theoretical optimism is not stimulated by the hard facts at all, which, taken by themselves, counsel caution. (There may be further reason for caution: owing to emerging incompatibilities between post-industrial progress and democracy as a system of government, the future of the system itself may be questioned in its geographical core.)[4] Rather, theoretical optimism, modest in itself, builds from a different and banal observation. Hard facts do not mean necessity. In political matters, particularly in matters of regime change, causal relations are only probable and outcomes uncertain. We can make broad probabilistic predictions about categories (such as, "Countries possessing quality X are more likely to develop democracy than . . ."), but we cannot make firm predictions about individual cases. In any single case, unless relevant circumstances cumulate in the extreme, the end result is not inescapable. This is true even if we were to discount the roles of choice and discretion in political events. But this role should not be discounted, especially when it comes to the macropolitical change embodied in regime crises and transitions. Not for nothing does the word *crisis* derive from the Greek *krisis,* meaning sorting out, choosing, deciding. From this to my next assertion the step is small.

It is a dismal science of politics (or the science of a dismal politics) that passively entrusts political change to exogenous and distant social transformations.[5] Applied to the future of democracy, such a science translates instinctively the structurally improbable (the hard facts) into the politically impossible. A recent carefully drawn propositional inventory of the conditions favoring the development or maintenance of democracy in the Third World lists forty-nine demanding conditions—mostly, in fact, preconditions.[6] A similarly lengthy list could have easily been drawn, after World War I, by a panel of European social scientists, Marxist or non-Marxist, to demonstrate the impossibility of a Communist revolution in backward places like czarist Russia. But

Lenin, by choosing to act, denied not only the prophecy but also his own social scientific Marxist heritage. And the Russian Revolution demanded new explanations.

Should we not, as students and advocates of democracy, reexamine our tried-and-true theoretical staple, to pare it down, to enrich and diversify it, somewhat? "It ill serves the cause of democracy in the third world," writes Myron Weiner, drawing from the Russian case,

> for countries to be told that their growth rates are too low, their political culture inappropriate for democracy to thrive, or that an independent judiciary, a free press, and political pluralism are alien to their political tradition. . . . Perhaps it is time to recognize that democratic theory, with its list of conditions and prerequisites, is a poor guide to action as well.[7]

Albert O. Hirschman's lifetime work has probably done the most to consistently expose the mechanisms by which existing paradigms—namely, theories about the conditions and prerequisites for economic and political development—can blind us to possible and even probable political action.[8]

Guillermo O'Donnell and Philippe Schmitter offer considerations on how to study democratic stability and change that buttress Weiner's and Hirschman's points.[9] Once democracy is established and functioning, democratic performance can be studied, to be sure, by reference to such enduring structures as class, party systems, prevailing values, or level of economic development[10] Social scientists refer to these structures in practicing what O'Donnell and Schmitter call normal social science methodology. But during periods of democratic transition and formation, those structures (whether or not they are themselves the agents of change) are called to respond to a changing situation. Quite apart from whether they are undergoing lasting mutations, they may at least temporarily cease to function as tried constraints or channels: interest perceptions may shift, class alliances may be suspended, party identities may lose their appeal, and cultural values and economic inequalities may be set aside.

In such a climate of uncertainty and potential reversals, initiative must come at a premium. Also, given uncertainty, how do structural and conjunctural factors recombine in the transition; to what extent are they recombined by actors; and how influential do structural factors remain? These issues do not appear to lend themselves to simple and parsimonious predictions. Constellations and permutations tend to become unique, and no set of them is exclusively and inherently superior when it comes to democratic success (more likely, a few may emerge as *reasonably* inferior). Thus, the realm of the possible, the plausible, indeed, the probable, can be expanded. I do not claim indeterminacy, but rather the need to explore further and to refuse to foreclose the search.

As many a reader may surmise, one recent democratic transition—that of Spain—could act as the midwife of the above reconsiderations. I remember distinctly the initial uneasiness among experts following the death of Francisco Franco. For the first two years, their attitude wavered consistently, intermittently afterwards, between withholding judgment and painting uncertain, mostly bleak scenarios. Everybody seemed to "know" that the transition would be difficult to call, and extremely delicate at any rate. But was there a social scientific ground to that assessment? In other words, why the uneasiness? To simplify matters, experts seemed to work more or less explicitly from two contrasting guides to prediction, loosely derived from existing democratic theory. The first guide augured well for Spanish democracy, by pointing to the fact that, during the last fifteen years of the dictatorship, the country had already progressed socially and economically, and in a laissez-faire context. The "Europeanization" of Spain stood in marked contrast, mentally, culturally, socially, from the more traditional and divided society that saw Franco's violent ascent to power. The other predictive guide argued the opposite: attempts at rapid regime changes are invariably traumatic and can backfire; but the more so if the old regime is still in place, is not rent by significant crises, and has in fact carefully arranged for, and committed itself to, an orderly succession. The two contradictory guides produced indeterminacy, the expert's unwillingness to issue a verdict. Or, if the expert were pressed, the latter guide would somehow prevail conservatively. Even my own dauntless attitude at the time was much less a matter of superior social science than of gut feelings and wishful thinking.

In the end, democracy succeeded and many analysts began to broaden their perspective. That is to say, the most important lesson we learned from that success was not that democratic and prosperous Europe had carried Spain along (for Spain's successful transition to democracy was, by itself, no proof that Europeanization had prevailed) but that our vision was too narrow. The scholars' early wavering and even pessimism stood in sharp contrast to the final success of Spain's transition. We have learned two lessons as a result. First, one limitation of existing social-change paradigms has been confirmed: to wit, that paradigms, though sharing social scientific ambitions, are competing or contrasting. Moreover, each paradigm, even when trying to overcome or recombine disparate predecessors, has predictive force only in those extreme, and therefore rare, occurrences when the positive (or negative) cumulate. This, incidentally, explains the social scientists' reluctance to predict events when questioned by the naive layperson. Second,

Spain's successful transition (and other, more complex, transitions) dramatically illustrated the role political actors may come to play in transitions where outcomes are indeterminate and available paradigms do not help.

In so doing, transitions such as Spain's revealed the essential reason for the experts' wavering between noncommittal and pessimistic assessments. In effect, we suffered from blind spots. We were inadequately prepared for the intervening role of political actors; inadequately prepared to perceive the extent to which innovative political action can contribute to democratic evolution; inadequately prepared, in sum, to entertain and give account of the notion that democracies can be made (or unmade) in the act of making them. Thus, we were taken by surprise when *reforma pactada*—a negotiated agreement between democratic forces and interests from the old regime—turned out to play a crucial role in carrying Spanish democratization over the top.

To be sure, nothing in this revaluation of transitions implies that they are easy affairs. This is certainly not the point of optimism. On the contrary, transitions are almost always demanding. Portugal, Argentina, and Spain held our attention precisely because nothing was foregone. Transitions, as crisis junctures, point to uncertain outcomes. Still, they also point to the need for action. The optimism—which is actually an open-mindedness—comes in connection with this latter aspect of transitions: that of decision and resolution.

Thus, as Juan Linz and Alfred Stepan have observed,[11] democratization is ultimately a matter of political crafting. By "crafting," I mean to describe chiefly four aspects of democratization: (1) the quality of the finished product (the particular democratic rules and institutions that are chosen among the many available);[12] (2) the mode of decision making leading to the selection of rules and institutions (pacts and negotiations versus unilateral action); (3) the type of "craftsmen" involved (the alliances and coalitions forged in the transition); and (4) the timing imposed on the various tasks and stages of the transition. Naturally, political actors in the transition may or may not have the objective opportunity—or the subjective ability that transcends opportunities—to make the correct choices. Nonetheless, it is these four aspects that ultimately influence the success of transitions.

The importance of crafting should be enhanced by Huntington's cautionary note about the future of democracy. When more countries arrive on the threshold of democracy without those structural or cultural qualities deemed important, when more arrive under conditions of harried and divisive mobilization, then the task of crafting should be the more crucial and challenging. Whatever the historical trends, whatever the hard facts, the importance of human action in a difficult transition should not be underestimated.[13]

A few words about how this essay will proceed. I will take the opposite tack to Robert Dahl's *Polyarchy*.[14] Dahl's justly popular book explores broad historical paths and general structural conditions for the development and maintenance of democracies. Only in a postscript to the book does the author tackle what we may call the "microproblems" of crafting. Further, the postscript opens on a cautionary note that foreshadowed the one issued by Huntington fifteen years later: "It is unrealistic to suppose, then, that there will be any dramatic change in the number of polyarchies within a generation or two."[15] Still, Dahl notes that, compared with most countries with profiles unfavorable to democracy (and very few with favorable ones), some countries have mixed profiles—that is, given the limits of existing strands of democratic theory, predictions are difficult to make. The purpose of the postscript is to explore policy and action recommendations that may help the democratization of the latter countries. But, in keeping with the very same theory which occupies most of *Polyarchy,* the recommendations are doubly restrained. First, they are limited to only one aspect of democratic crafting: the choice of rules and institutions that reconcile cohesive democratic government with strong mutual guarantees for conflicting groups. Second, unless a country has a highly favorable profile, the recommendations advise against pushing for rapid democratization, even in a power vacuum. For institution building takes time, and so does habituation to the conventions of new democratic institutions. Beyond this, Dahl's recommendations contain little of any use, as he himself points out, for those aspects of democratic crafting that relate to processes, timing, alliances, and in sum tactics.

My essay intends, instead, to look mainly beyond the existing strands of theory; to extend and improve Dahl's list of recommendations; and to give democratization a second chance. Questioning Huntington's hard facts and Dahl's theories behind those facts is therefore only a small part of my task. Our blind spots about the role of crafting reflect the penchant of social scientists to consider regime transitions as a kind of black box—interchangeable steps to a foreclosed outcome—rather than open processes of interaction. Worse, in close connection with that methodological penchant, our blind spots also give a distorted and somehow dispiriting view of democracy as a particularly rare and delicate plant that cannot be transplanted. This view of democracy will be corrected in the next chapter. But the preliminary exercise will take us only a small part of the way.

From there, the focus will shift to the hitherto overlooked politics of transitions. This occupies chapters 3–5. They will take up in turn the insufficiently stressed rewards that the democratic game, as an open contest, can offer to those who come to play it; the rules that are best suited to induce reluctant players to play, and the transitional coalitions that favor the adoption of those rules; and finally the tactics (bearing on the speed of transitions and on trade-offs between regimes and oppositions) that assist democratization. Supported by evidence from recent transitions, these chapters should insert themselves in the cracks, as it were, left open by existing democratic theory. In so doing, the "cracks" will get magnified and more visible. They will accommodate possibilities that seemed squeezed out of the realm of democratic development as commonly understood. In the process, the predicament envisioned by Dahl and Huntington should not appear quite as forbidding.

In turn, the treatment of transitions will raise novel questions about what lies beyond transitions. Will a difficult transition weigh heavily on the future of a democracy? How heavily? Or, to rephrase the question, are the problems that are said to afflict new democracies (i.e., performance authenticity, so-called legitimacy) invariably brought on by difficult transitions? In particular, are contemporary transitions marred by a socially conservative bias without which they could not succeed? Also, if the problems of a new democracy bring about a breakdown, in what precise way can the breakdown be explained by the circumstances of its birth, or by its sheer newness—except to say that everything that comes after must somehow be explained by what existed before?

Should we assume as well that, because almost any democratic transition is difficult, a long period of time is needed, way past the transition proper, before a new democracy is safe? That is, does a new democracy require a protracted process of "consolidation" (to use a popular but fuzzy term)? Does it require the testing and validation over time of new institutions and untried rules? What, otherwise, are the exact risks of decay and breakdown? And what do we make of the broader philosophy (embodied in Dahl's postscript) behind these concerns with consolidation; namely, that democratization should be a slow process, offering opportunities for fuller development and orderly internalization of democratic skills?

Finally, is what we call legitimacy anything more than behavioral compliance, and does it need to be anything more? In point of fact, and until I justify the use, I will employ "legitimacy," "loyalty," and similar terms in the simple sense of behavioral compliance.

In sum, all the above aspects of democratic theory also need a second and more critical look. Chapters 6 and 7 take up the assignment.

I conclude the essay by returning to the hard facts and how they bear on the future of democracy. Are more democracies possible? In answer, chapter 8 will consider how, thanks to crises whose outcomes appear indeterminate, crafting may operate (or has operated) with success even in countries and regimes whose predicament would not otherwise be favorable. Interestingly, the differences among the countries and regimes I have chosen to examine—mainly those of Central America and Eastern Europe—do not prevent the possibility of similar outcomes. Finally, chapter 9 will return to the theme of chapter 2 in considering the role of international factors in favoring (or hindering) present and impending democratizations. Important as domestic historical and structural conditions may be for these processes, it is sufficient to reflect on the role of regional and global hegemons such as the United States and the Soviet Union to appreciate the weight that diffusion and demonstration effects exercise, more and more so, on political transformations that today embrace entire regions of the globe. This insight, too, is in keeping with the consciously actor-oriented approach of the essay.

Antonio Gramsci, in some ways a Leninist with an eye for the power that political persuasion exercises in the construction of new regimes, spoke in reference to goal-oriented action of a pessimism of the intelligence rescued by an optimism of the will. My essay is cast in that mold.

Before beginning, I would like to make a confession and to offer an encouragement to the readers. The confession is that my reflections, my examples, will be influenced by my knowledge of Western Europe. The burden of the proof, in extrapolating to the larger picture, is on me. Not a light burden because my reflections go beyond Western and Western-inspired societies to embrace Communist societies as well. In this regard, there is no hiding it, I have obliged events. Originally, the essay was to focus mainly on transitions from right-wing dictatorships, with a final chapter essaying to apply the same type of insights to still unattempted transitions from communism. But, during the drafting stage, mounting events in the Soviet Union and Poland, and anticipations of similar events in Hungary, encouraged me to make my comparisons more integral to the essay. Even at this early point, the comparisons between transitions East and West reveal common issues and behaviors that are the more striking in view of the institutional differences between the respective regimes of each area.

The encouragement to the readers is for them to read the notes at the end of the essay. Most are integral to the argument. Some are entertaining.

CHAPTER II

On Diffusion
How Democracy Can Grow
in Many Soils

Is democracy a hothouse plant? Can it be transplanted? It might be useful to recast the image as one of transferring, not plants, but loyalties. Is it difficult to transfer loyalties from a nondemocratic to a democratic regime? The answer is: less difficult than we think, if we construe loyalty as mere behavioral compliance, and if we reflect on the calculus of transferral. But before reflecting, which we will do in the next chapter, we need to clarify our definition of democracy. We also need a longer treatment of the birthplace and diffusion routes of modern democracy to show that smallness of birthplace and checkered routes are in part responsible for the artful hothouse image.

For all its historical and geographical ups and downs, diffusion remains a key (nowadays writ large) ingredient of democratic development. Thus, democratization may be helped by the suppliers (advanced democracies, regional or global powers) as much as by the consumers. Similarly, it may also be helped by the attractiveness of the imported product and the consumer's willingness or need to become worthy of the product as much as by some inborn fitness of that consumer. New democracies are thus less the result of cumulative, necessary, predictable, and systematic developments than of historical busts and booms, global opinion climates, shifting opportunities, and contingent preferences. And such is the context, open to human intervention, within which the transfer of loyalties will best be made sense of.

WHAT DEMOCRACY?

The emphasis on diffusion demands a descriptive and historically bounded definition of democracy. The object of diffusion and implementation is not a normative analytical entity—an abstract construct assembled from a set of axiomatic standards about democracy.[1] It is instead a concrete fact, with history and geography behind it. It is a set of already tested and strictly political institutions and practices, rules, and procedures from which a number of otherwise diverse countries we thus call "democratic" have variously borrowed over time in order to govern themselves. It is to this pool of specifics, and not to an abstract, that political actors in a transition react today in a variety of ways: by deferring to them; by selecting from them; by improvising, innovating, inventing upon them. It is to this pool, and not to an abstract, that concrete actors may turn at one concrete point for one convenient purpose—in essence, setting up government in diversity as a way of defusing conflict.

I doubt whether that pool of practices and institutions, rules, and procedures can also secure some other objective, other goods, higher standards of life, economic democracy, equality, the perfect citizen, self-fulfillment. The evidence (but what is "evidence" of self-fulfillment, or even of economic democracy?) is not clear. For example, available if limited systematic evidence indicates that, in policy areas other than civil rights and personal freedoms, existing democracies do not necessarily perform better, or worse, than nondemocratic regimes.[2] It is therefore ill-advised to conflate democracy with a set of elusive ultimate objectives and normative standards—coveted as they are.

There is another reason to avoid conflation. Democracy may well be sought by some actors and at some points in history for ulterior objectives, directly or nebulously connected (depending on their vagueness) to the pursuit of a higher societal design. But if the first objective is not or does not soon become coexistence in diversity, it is then axiomatic that the democratic experiment will be short-lived. The achievement of mutual survival could be positively affected by the presence of some of the other objectives. But interference with it is also possible. It is equally possible that the latter objectives will ultimately be sacrificed to the former. These are empirical, not definitional, issues. For purposes of definition, therefore, political democracy, as the issue in the transitions, is understood in the conventional Schumpeterian or representative sense.[3] The emphasis is on free and universal suffrage in a context of civil liberties, on competitive parties, on the selection of alternative candidates for office, and on the presence of political institutions that regulate and guarantee the roles of government and opposition.

WHAT DIFFUSION?

Modern representative democracy was born in a small, maritime, insular corner of Western Europe[4] under converging circumstances whose uniqueness cannot be overemphasized.[5] Among the unique circumstances, scholars have investigated the rise of the rule of law and constitutionalism, the presence of a politically relevant liberal public opinion, Protestantism, the weakness of absolutism (or a special balance between royal prerogatives and estate liberties), the smallness of the peasantry, the commercialization of agriculture, a strong entrepreneurial bourgeoisie, ethnic-religious homogeneity, early industrialization, a co-optable working class, elite competitive politics predating the expansion of suffrage, the slow and deliberate extension of the latter (democracy on the installment plan), and so forth.

The list explains democracy's hothouse image, but is it inclusive and exclusive? Was democracy not intended for export?[6] In effect, the unrepeatability of those circumstances can also be turned on its head: to wit, just as the circumstances surrounding the birth of modern democracy were unique, another unique cluster of circumstances could account for the adoption of that same democracy elsewhere—perhaps precisely by diffusion. There is no compelling logic against this line of reasoning. Unique circumstances are not the same as requisite circumstances, and fortuitous outcomes are not the same as nonrepeatable outcomes.

Thus, if democracy was fortuitous in its cradle,[7] why then should it not be fortuitous elsewhere? Why should paths to democracy elsewhere necessarily replicate a first path, or fail if unable to?[8] Indeed, the striking and confounding fact is that once democracy was born, its exclusive pedigree did not prevent its diffusion. On the contrary, it encouraged diffusion and emulation, spotty and unpredictable as they have proved to be. One force at play was democracy's special association with the idea of social progress.

Social progress (the kind of economic, intellectual, sociocultural, and politicocultural conditions that took root in the northwestern corner of Europe between the eighteenth and ninteenth centuries) was originally seen as the cause of democracy: curbing stagnant arbitrariness and propelling humankind toward a more perfect and righteous self-rule.

But, over time, the social potentials of political democracy as a more perfect self-rule became more and more salient and captivating, at least in the eyes of aspiring elites from politically "backward" societies.[9] So the order of events was reversed. A demonstration effect set in: political reform was now expected to produce that social progress on which its advent had originally been predicated.[10]

Demonstration effects began in the ninteenth century in the immediate geographical or politicocultural periphery of Western Europe: east-central Europe, southern Europe, and by way of the latter, Latin America.[11] As they expanded beyond the immediate periphery and moved into the twentieth century, demonstration effects were joined by a new force, namely, the direct exportation of democracy by democratic powers with global, regional, or colonial clout. Thus, diffusion became progressively more central to democratic development.

Still, diffusion continued to encounter serious difficulties, even devastating reversals, as it proceeded. For one thing, the ideal attractiveness of democracy and its demonstration potentials were not always helped by the rise of advanced democracies to international status. World War I, the crowning affirmation of democracies as global powers, was simultaneously the force behind democracy's greatest burst and its greatest crisis. In the 1920s, 1930s, and 1940s, democracy as an ideal and a global force for benevolent progress suffered its greatest challenge at the hand of new forms of authoritarianism and totalitarianism. For another thing, even when the international context was favorable to democracy, there remained the problem of receptivity to democracy by the host country. After World War II the defeat of fascism and decolonization offered the correct international conditions. Democracy returned to defeated and liberated countries in the West; optimism surrounded the introduction of democracy in formerly colonial countries. But that optimism was fairly soon confounded by the failure of most new countries to accommodate the Western model of representative democracy.

Whatever the explanations for these Third World failures, they gave credit during trying times for democracies to a line of theoretical pessimism:[12] if democracy was chancy in its origins, then it must be even more so in its replicas. Yet the reverse of this broadly unassailable statement is that the availability of the first democratic examples, chancy in themselves, also made reinventing democracy (reinventing the wheel) unnecessary. On this faintly Veblenian plane, the plane of global political trends, those first examples made democracy elsewhere *less* chancy. From this comes the unmistakable weight, limits notwithstanding, of demonstration effects.

But more can be said in favor of demonstration effects. True, conflicting trends, booms and busts, changing opinion climates and worldviews, have marked, at times in short order, democratic diffusion in the twentieth century. There is, however, a silver lining in this. For underneath those shifts in directions and opinion climates, I detect a promising trend for the future of democracy. This trend (whose implications have largely escaped the attention of social scientists) consists in the emergence among political practitioners of a more realistic assessment, already gleaned in postwar Europe but clearer and more global today, of what makes democracy's performance as a concrete system of government attractive, at least more attractive than other tested systems. It appears that the void left by the long-faded view of democracy as a universal key to material progress is being filled by a new appreciation of its pristine and unique virtue as protection against the oppression of arbitrary and undivided rule.[13]

This rediscovery, in turn, owes much to the emerging realization that, if democracy is not the key to progress, then neither were those alternative regimes that came to replace democracy, claiming superior performance and indeed a superior concept of humankind.[14]

In Europe and Japan between the two world wars, the loss of faith in the regenerative virtues of Western democracy opened the door to authoritarian and totalitarian regimes that would soon leave the host countries in shambles. Authoritarian regimes that survived World War II—even when doing a creditable job with material progress by liberalizing their economies (Spain)—came to be perceived as an ultimate obstacle to that very progress. In colonial countries that achieved nationhood after the war, the forceful replacement of early democratic experiments by nondemocratic regimes was not accompanied, to say the least, by any visible improvement in any facet of regime performance. In Latin America, political see-saws, especially frequent after World War II, revealed how even military regimes with progressive agendas—and most nondemocratic regimes had only negative agendas—could not hold on to them long, exclusively, or persuasively enough to legitimize themselves. Moreover, issues of legitimacy, based on new criteria of performance, have been surfacing among those exceptional cases of orderly material success in a nondemocratic context, which are the newly industrializing countries of East Asia. And finally, Communist regimes, even after halting their worst oppressions, are now foundering precisely on the complete failure of their agenda for social progress. Thus, they are now harking back to models of progress, and even to political models, with a Western tinge.

The inviability of most of these regimes on their own terms, as command economies presumably more capable of rallying and concentrating resources than ostensibly dispersive democracies, has served over the years to remove the invidious comparison. If social progress is not a criterion for choosing democracy (because it would instigate excessive expectations),[15] then neither is it one for discarding it.

But there is more. Beyond the social failures of non-democratic regimes there is the revealed horror—not a failure, but a fulfillment—of these regimes as human oppressors and community disorganizers. Here the relentless brutalities of Nazism and of Latin American dictatorships, of Russian and Eastern European Stalinism, of China's Great Leap Forward and Cultural Revolution, different as they are, have come to stand out as their victims come to contemplate whether *(and how)* to pursue democracy. Brutality—unrelieved (if it could ever be relieved) by other achievements—revealed not only the essence of the regimes but also just how democracy in its concrete incarnations has always been ultimately superior. It has been superior as a system to curb oppression; to reassert, as a matter of self-interest, mutual coexistence; to reconstitute a community; and to reestablish a sense of personal worth and public dignity.[16] In this sense, democracy, limited as it may be in its social achievements, can emerge as incomparably preferable to dictatorship.

This is not to suggest that the appreciation of democracy's innate virtues is sufficient to remove obstacles to democratic diffusion,[17] or that a majority of significant actors now share this appreciation, or that (if shared) it would come with an invariably clear blueprint for establishing democracy. I wish to point out only that a greater appreciation of democracy's worth, coupled with a lowering of expectations in regard to its material achievements, is beneficial in at least two ways.

First, as I mentioned in the first page of this chapter, democracy's attractiveness may stir the prospective "consumer" to become worthy of the product, to change as it were his consumption habits. It should be clear that a prudential and "satisficing" view of democracy as a system that curbs oppression and reconstitutes a community shattered or left adrift by dictatorship does not exempt from but encourages political crafting. Such crafting is evident in the attention to constitutional design and the latitude afforded diverse political parties and constituencies in reconstituting postwar European democracies and in more recent transitions in southern Europe and South America. More generally, greater investment in crafting (so as consciously to steer clear of repeated authoritarian involutions) can open novel possibilities for democracy in contexts previously deemed unfavorable. Contemporary predemocratic developments in Eastern European countries, involving negotiations between regime and opposition, suggest as much.

Second, one factor that reconciles to democracy reluctant political actors tied to the previous regime is that in the inaugural phase coexistence usually takes precedence over any radical social and economic programs. Such precedence stems from understanding the limits of democratic (and other) politics as natural harbingers of material progress. It stems as well from a fuller appreciation that willfully using democracy as a Jacobin tool of progress not only is ingenuous but also may raise intolerable political risks; namely, authoritarian backlashes and, in anticipation, escalation into a virtuous "guided" democracy.

Past democracies—the most instructive example from the 1930s being the second Spanish republic—have foundered on such Jacobin instincts, or even on impressions of such instincts. By giving reform precedence over coexistence and making support for reform the test of legitimacy, they have unintentionally fulfilled a prophecy: the losers would be unwilling to reconcile themselves to a nascent democracy.[18] The example looms large among political practitioners in Europe and Latin America.[19] Indeed, the importance of coexistence has not gone unnoticed, despite its significant policy sacrifices, by those who still sympathize ideally with a more Jacobin democracy.[20]

I have depicted democracy's disengagement from the idea of social progress as a silver lining because it has actually given democracy more realistic, more sturdily conscious grounds for claiming superiority in the eyes of public opinion and political practitioners. It has also increased interest in democratic crafting. To some social scientists—accustomed to relying on objective quantitative evidence—the reactions of public opinion and political practitioners will unfortunately seem less than a silver lining: perhaps a straw in the wind, perhaps a mere will-o'-the-wisp. Indeed, there is an interesting divorce between the reactions of political practitioners and public opinion and those of social scientists to the message that democracy may not bring about social progress.

A METHODOLOGICAL AND CULTURAL NOTE

In the social sciences, the reaction has been a shift in paradigms of democratic development, in order to recapture solid terrain and to reassert the primacy of structurally grounded theory. The paradigmatic shift picked up momentum in the 1960s following the failure of former colonial countries to develop their economies *and* sustain democratization. Before then, the paradigms of modernization (or political development, or democratization) that prevailed on American campuses still had late developers replicating the path to development set by the first European countries (in practice, England). Late developers could actually learn from early developers, though often with much greater difficulty, and could even use shortcuts, so as to finally consolidate social progress and democratic outcomes. In this sense, the paradigms were models of transitional societies moving toward

modernity *cum* democracy. They were neoclassical or neo-
liberal, in Andrew Janos's words; they were functionalist and
therefore both teleological and implicitly optimistic;[21] and
they often made room for the ultimately positive effects of
international demonstration.[22] But once the optimism fostered by the riveting wave of decolonization was gone, two
new lines of analysis came to the fore:

1. On one line, diffusion and, in particular, demonstration effects were eclipsed by a surge of interest in domestic
sociostructural prerequisites for (and therefore impediments
to) political development. One case in point is the revival of
the hothouse view of democracy—a view that was never fully
discarded—by a series of studies (for a few years, a burgeon-
ing intellectual industry) on the economic and structural
preconditions for democracy.[23] The same attention to domestic structures is found in paradigms that shifted the
analysis away from democracy and postulated instead the
rise of various nondemocratic alternatives to mobilize scarce
domestic resources and guide them out of backwardness. In
both types of paradigms, but especially the latter, the significance, if any, of international demonstration—in particular,
the attempt to shortcut paths to development—is that of introducing nearly insurmountable social strains and disorganization, which nondemocratic mobilizational regimes are
called to address and correct.

2. On another, somewhat later, line of analysis (especially
popular with students of Latin America), diffusion effects
have instead become more decisive but decidedly more negative. Various paradigms of *dependencia* and bureaucratic
authoritarianism postulated that rampant stagnation and
authoritarian involutions in the Third World and Latin
America were more than manifestations of nearly insurmountable social strains, for which the demonstration ef-

fects of advanced industrial democracies were at most indirectly responsible. They were the direct result of a global economic order wished, in the interest of their own survival, by those democracies.

Two aspects of the paradigm shifts—one methodological, one cultural-professional—deserve emphatic repetition. In the first place, the shifts add status precisely to those cumulative, vicious circle paradigms whose critique by Albert Hirschman I mentioned in the introductory chapter. Even when the paradigms do not rule out democracy—as in the literature that concentrates on prerequisites for democracy—its achievement is at best projected in a foggy and theoretically irrelevant future against which prevailing odds conspicuously conspire. In the second place, the paradigms show a singular cultural-professional insensitivity, with methodological consequences, for the issue of whether the human repression systematically pursued by modern dictatorships can be self-defeating. Those paradigms that postulated the viability of mobilizational models for the Third World did so on the heels of European fascism.[24] They did so even as their examples of mobilization were failing in most developing countries for lack of anything but the most rhetorical blueprints for development.

My qualm is not the moral obtuseness of these paradigms, as their inattention to whether systematic repression, by itself, can produce anything, including its own perpetuation. The qualm is not dissimilar when it comes to those paradigms which, eschewing mobilizational models, looked instead at authoritarianism as itself part agent and part symptom of spiraling decay. Those paradigms were nevertheless just as disinclined, by their similar commitment to the logic of vicious circles, to ponder the same "intangible"; namely, whether and how the cumulation of unspeakable repression can induce the victims to act politically in a regime crisis (and some crises had already occurred) to undo the vicious circle.

In sum, the contrast between the reactions of political scientists and political practitioners to the faltering of democratic diffusion should be clear. On the side of political science, we have seen a more concerted effort to find more scientifically correct explanations for, to make greater sense out of, this faltering. On the side of politics, we have, today, growing signs of a more conscious search for democratic political crafting, so as to deny the new scientific prophecies.[25]

CHAPTER III

Why Transferring Loyalties to Democracy May Be Less Difficult Than We Think

One argument of the last chapter was that an incentive to transfer loyalties to democracy stems, especially nowadays, from a better appreciation of democracy's original meaning as a system of coexistence in diversity. At the beginning of the same chapter I also stated that if, during a transition to democracy, the first object is not or does not soon become coexistence, it is axiomatic that the democratic experiment will be short-lived. Thus the incentive becomes an imperative. The present chapter treats both aspects separately, to the extent that they are separable. In treating coexistence as an incentive, I will delve more deeply into the sources of its attractiveness. In treating it as an imperative, I will show why and how crafting, as a range of strategies and institutional solutions, can (and must) be employed to realize that attractiveness in the transition.

Because the two exercises are largely conceptual, references to concrete examples will be few, and limited to illustration. My aim is to demonstrate that difficult democratizations can still be helped; to disprove democracy's image as a hothouse plant; to advance, in sum, a "minimalist" view of democracy. I leave for later treatments the empirical questions of whether political actors in recent transitions have actually behaved to fulfill democracy's promise, and whether objective conditions prior to or proper to specific transitions influence such behavior.

TRANSFERRING LOYALTIES: INCENTIVES AND REQUIREMENTS

The idea that coexistence is a basic component of democracy is not new. In *Polyarchy*, Robert Dahl speaks of the need for mutual security, without which, by definition, government and opposition can hardly tolerate each other. There are, however, two ways of examining the chances that a system of mutual security, or coexistence, will develop. One way does not exclude the other, but they deserve sorting out. The first way is to ask, with Dahl, the classic question: "What circumstances significantly increase the mutual security of government and opposition[?]"[1] And by "circumstances" he means objective conditions, prerequisites, and impediments. In sum, he asks whether (for example) the structure of inequalities, subcultural cleavages, or national traits act to reduce conflict in a democratic context and make mutual toleration more likely.[2] The second way is to ask what makes coexistence attractive—difficult though it may be. What situations emerge in the crisis of a dictatorship or in a transition that would make coexistence an appealing choice? The two perspectives can employ remarkably distinct logical strands; hence they tend to organize the same raw variables in different combinations.

The former perspective looks at the costs of *having* democracy; it asks whether diversity can be afforded in objectively conflictive societies. The underlying assumption is that democracy will bring about new conflict, sufficient in some cases to prevent coexistence. The latter perspective reverses the former and borders on the ultimate question: can a country afford *not* to have coexistence? In so doing, it probes the periphery of what we usually consider possible in matters of democratic development. Behind the reversal of perspectives is a view of democracy as a more efficient way of defusing and regulating serious inherited conflict. Therefore, there is also the view that the shift to democracy involves choice (predicated on *perceptions* of conflict).

In sum, the first perspective is mainly concerned with impediments to coexistence, with what presumably makes democracy impossible, not with what brings it about. Within this perspective, a country's apparent lack of long-standing impediments to coexistence cannot explain, when taken alone, why at one point that country chooses it. The central concern in the second perspective is instead the choice, the decision, to overcome impediments if necessary.[3]

In essence, this is also Dankwart Rustow's concern. "A people who were not in conflict about some rather fundamental matters," he writes, "would have little need to devise democracy's elaborate rules for conflict regulation."[4] Rustow goes on to explain that political actors are motivated to elaborate those rules by the desire to terminate (or forestall)[5] an inconclusive struggle for regime supremacy. In other words, Rustow's "conflict about fundamental matters" is something that arises, or threatens to arise, within the old regime. Whatever one may say about the historical accuracy of Rustow's characterization, it possesses an unquestionably familiar ring vis-à-vis contemporary transitions from authoritarianism to democracy. As we will see in a moment, such transitions always unfold from a crisis of legitimacy that the old regime cannot resolve or reabsorb by whatever available and acceptable means.

Rustow's characterization is also promising. It follows from it that democracy's rules, being a means for coexistence, need not be more than a second best for the parties that negotiate their adoption. Rules can be a matter of instrumental agreement worked out among competing leaderships, even in the absence of a popular or elite consensus on fundamentals. To paraphrase Rustow, the acceptance of democracy's rules is not a prerequisite because their elaboration may well be integral to the transition itself.[6] It follows, in sum, that genuine democrats need not precede democracy,[7] and that the transfer of loyalties from dictatorship to democracy does not require exceptionally favorable circumstances. Ultimately, the viability of a new democracy can rest on making the transfer appealing, convenient, or compelling. Ultimately, it can rest on its attractiveness relative to its alternatives.

This is not to deny the benefits of favorable circumstances. Arguably, such circumstances as a rooted democratic culture and social tolerance fostered by limited class inequalities or by ethnic and national homogeneity augur well for a democratic transition. But they are not necessary.[8] It behooves me to reiterate that the emphasis on democracy as a relative choice is to explore the periphery of what is possible in countries that are otherwise structurally or culturally not "ripe" for democracy. After all, it appears that even among those early democracies born under the best circumstances, hardly one was born without double-talk, self-interested calculations, even resistance from its very practitioners. Hardly one was born because genuine democrats existed in any decisive number. Yet, one way or another, they were born, and often prospered unscathed.

Still, how can democracy be made to endure? It is time to approach coexistence from another side, not as an attractive reason for embracing democracy in principle, but as a central objective in any transition, lest there be no embrace at all. But the objective is indeed taxing, nearly always demanding an exacting series of tasks and priorities. A dictatorial regime embroiled in, or moving toward, an inconclusive struggle may well suffer a loss of legitimacy, yet it will not, because of this alone, lose to democracy.[9] Nor will it lose to democracy just because democracy's vaunted superiority in reconstituting a political community gathers appreciation in principle. The objective also demands the emergence of a concretely attractive set of democratic rules that are designed to replace that struggle with coexistence. Without these rules, the claims often voiced by authoritarian leaders ("Our country is not ripe for democracy") may hold sway. That is, democracy's vaunted superiority must begin to take concrete, operative, testable shape. This is more than a tautology because it is precisely at this juncture that the challenge of agreeing upon the right rules is found.

The following two sections take up two reasons for the challenge. Typically, recent (and prospective) regime crises rarely make a clean break with the past. The first section discusses this reality. The second addresses the fact that the essence of the democratic method (the other side of coexistence), is to regulate and institutionalize uncertainty of outcomes.[10] The two reasons yield the following observations: reluctant players of the prospective democratic game who are called to renounce alternatives may find it initially difficult to see what (if anything) they actually stand to gain from coexistence. Thus, the challenge of democratic transitions is that they are compelled to work within uncertain parameters and to build a sort of borrowed or presumptive legitimacy.[11] In simpler words, by choosing the democratic method, and therefore transferring loyalties or bestowing legitimacy on democracy, political actors are also choosing a degree of calculated uncertainty.

In some cases, the calculation is relaxed by a surge of

democratic sentiments, buttressed perhaps by the contemplation of authoritarianism's dismal record. But frequently such surges are not sufficiently swift, strong, and widespread, or so stably motivated, to make democracy a foregone conclusion. Often, therefore, people will be less generous about extending trust.[12] This is where crafting becomes important. It makes institutionalized uncertainty palatable and indeed rewarding, and hence stable in the long run. In a few cases crafting should be reasonably careful; in most others it should be very careful. The latter cases are the most instructive.

ON REGIME CRISES

The record of democratizations shows that just about the easiest, almost surgical, method of replacing modern dictatorship with democracy has been war and occupation. But the record also shows that the method has been quite unusual. Further, the method will unlikely be employed in the future. In contrast, all recent classifications and typologies of democratic transitions—designed to systematize typical paths to democratization—reveal that the most numerous types involve coming to terms domestically with, and accommodating in some form, residues from the past regime.[13] This is particularly true of typologies dealing with more recent transitions, which frequently arise from efforts within the old regime to extricate itself from crisis.

Defeat and occupation by democratic superpowers have historically created particularly favorable circumstances for democracy, in that they have tended to make a clean break with the past. The four classic cases in this group (Germany, Italy, Japan, and Austria) all experienced a devastating failure in their adoption of fascism, one of the two most ambitious antidemocratic models in contemporary history. But their common experience also makes them historically idiosyncratic. The point is best illustrated by Nazi Germany. Given Nazism's totalitarian mobilization in pursuit of a global millennium, its utter defeat, only twelve years after the Nazis came to power, could not but leave a total organizational and power vacuum, a sense of apocalyptic and self-induced demise, and an ingrained rejection of any new totalitarian experiment. For all that the Allied occupational forces and the Germans did to purge the country of its legacy and to build strong democratic institutions, Nazism's own failure made it easier to obliterate that legacy to begin with.[14]

However, short of the Nazi-type holocaust that I just depicted—brought upon a dictatorship by its own wars of self-fulfillment—it is unlikely that the crisis of a dictatorship is so total as to leave a perfect vacuum of interests, organizations, and loyalties that a new democracy can occupy unannounced.[15] To be sure, as I have stressed in my discussion of democratic diffusion, the demise of fascism has cast general discredit on dictatorships. Moreover, the discrediting has been strengthened by the recent collapse, final or in process, of other repressive models in Latin America (bureaucratic authoritarianism) and in the Communist world. These failures have revealed how dictatorships, when left to their own devices, are often incapable of reacting to or anticipating crises—so as to reabsorb them—in ways that are not uninformed, convulsive, inflexible, or repressive.[16] Underneath this incapacity, they have revealed the tendency of dictatorships toward entropy and obsolescence, given the rigidities of their founding ideologies and purposes. In sum, the record shows that dictatorships do not endure.

But, on the way out, neither do they leave a perfect vacuum. In fact, their inherent incapacities have not been lost on contemporary authoritarian elites. Even in the Communist world the elites have recently shown less cohesiveness or single-mindedness than their earlier European models. That is one reason why recent crises (and, I would venture, future ones) are progressively either rooted or ushering in indigenous efforts in the regime to extricate itself. Paradoxically, therefore, despite any discredit, the legacy of despotism cannot be removed surgically, but requires some difficult reconciliation.

The typical scenario unfolds as follows: regimes faced with a crisis will seek reequilibration, possibly through repression, to resolve the crisis. However, efforts at reequilibration/repression, which are traditionally costly and inconclusive, do not meet with unanimous regime support. In fact, the crisis may itself be ultimately rooted in institutional conflict or generational discontinuity inside the regime about its purposes and its instruments.[17] Under such circumstances, the next step in the crisis (at least a typical step in moving toward democracy) may well be extrication. But extrication demands some counterparts before the transition takes a democratic direction.

To put it somewhat differently, what starts as an effort by members of the old elite to rescue the status quo may take an unintended direction as other members of the elite, with more innovative dispositions, join in.[18] Given the volatility of regime crisis, such changes in disposition should not be surprising. I suggest in the introductory chapter that "normal social science methodology" does not apply to regime crises and regime transitions in general. Structural explanations for behavior and performance become, as it were, suspended. Even if we assume that the group interests of the actors in a crisis (in the present case, actors from the old regime) remain "the same," group behavior becomes contingent, for all but the most hardened believers, on perceptions of costs, success, and the behavior of others. In sum, group behavior may crumble. That is why action intended to stonewall change may next attract action to extricate one-self.

These remarks about changing group behavior are perti-nent vis-à-vis right-wing authoritarian regimes; they need some adjustment when it comes to Communist post-totali-tarian regimes.[19] Unlike totalitarian regimes, authoritarian ones do not exercise command through new and ruthless institutions of their own (the single party as an organiza-tional and pedagogical weapon). Rather, they make do by penetrating and co-opting traditional formations and insti-tutions—armies, bureaucracies, regular courts, incorporated economic interests—with which they maintain an ambigu-ous relationship, often one of convenience. Also, they are often military regimes; and because military regimes see themselves as *régimes d'exception,* they are sensitive to con-flict internal to the military institution between exceptional/political and stable/corporate roles.

Authoritarian regimes have therefore recently evinced a proclivity to deteriorate through self-exhaustion. Without having necessarily done anything irreparable to doom them-selves they become, by the nature of their closed system, sluggish, inefficient, unable to adjust to changing times, and irrelevant. Or by liberalizing, in order to reequilibrate them-selves, they trigger higher expectations; or they substantially alter the place occupied by some of their organized consti-tuencies; or they show an inability to resolve the crisis of confidence that typically accompanies the death or inca-pacitation of the first dictator; or, if a military junta leads the regime, they are sooner or later confronted with inter-secting, inter-service and military-political conflicts, espe-cially in the event of some foreign policy misadventure.

It is not necessary to impose order on these disparate sig-nals of crisis—to weave them into one or another testable chain of causality—to appreciate that each of these chains can, in its own special way, lead to "secession": forces that are part of the coalitions supporting or running a dictatorship may come to consider the regime expendable and be tempted to abandon it. We have, then, a strategic context in which old forces and interests are changing their attitude toward the extant regime yet themselves will not disappear.

In order to turn this situation into a democratic transition, the task is to make the change of attitudes stable. If the regime is set aside, then the transition should be, not a temporary retreat awaiting better times (a typical phenomenon in Latin America), but an actual transfer of loyalties. The challenge is how to reconcile those forces and interests to a democratic compromise while, at a minimum, removing those structures that are incompatible with political democracy. The challenge, to be explored in the next chapter, is *how* to fulfill Dahl's famous axiom, as reformulated at the beginning of the chapter, that a competitive regime is more likely to emerge if tolerance is made less costly than maintaining a repressive system.

Post-totalitarian (i.e., Communist) regimes, unlike authoritarian ones, have inherited a single party and an ideology that traditionally play a more exclusive role in guiding society and bureaucratic and economic institutions. But the party and the ideology have been losing their grip, distinctiveness, and purpose. This explains the crises and attempted extrications, the content and motives of which are not that different nowadays from those of authoritarian regimes. Common to both, for instance, are programmatic and policy obsolescence and (China, Romania) the problem of succession. Nonetheless, extrications in post-totalitarian regimes meet special difficulties that might stymie them before they trespass into democratization. Given the party's persistent role, post-totalitarian regimes, unlike authoritarian ones, have not allowed any latitude for the constituencies and institutions that serve or coalesce around them. Yet, this ambiguous, even semipluralist, latitude could be one significant force in helping and possibly triggering secession. This means that efforts to change Communist post-totalitarian regimes more often take the form of extrication guided by the very core of the regime than that of lateral secession proper. And this is what makes trespassing into democratization more difficult to predict—yet possibly easier to guide if and when a threshold has finally been passed and the regimes set themselves to the task.

It might seem to some readers that I have given excessive importance to the ability of an obsolescent regime to survive the jettisoning of its political machinery, and that I have underplayed the democratic opposition's ability to dispose of that past more radically. But I must insist that the role of democrats in the crisis of dictatorship is rather special and is constrained in some typical ways. There are important variations from case to case (for example, popular democratic opposition is showing a surprising and unique resilience in Eastern Europe). Moreover, democrats—it is a central point of the essay—are quite capable of gathering resources and credibility as democratic transitions unfold and civil society is politically reconstituted. It is at these later stages that democracy's capacity to emerge as a superior option shows itself at its best. But the role played by the democratic opposition and civil society generally in triggering and directing the very first stages of regime crises is another matter. Even when the opposition has maintained some degree of underground organization and coordination, even when socially rooted partisan loyalties show resilience under the regime, it seems to me that the role of the opposition is at least almost never sufficient.

The violent overthrow of dictatorship by its own domestic enemies, and nothing else, is already a rare occurrence.

Government inability to meet force with force frequently hides the internal dissolution of the dictatorship.[20] The overthrow at the hands of democrats in particular, whether by peaceful mobilization or by conventional revolt, seems even rarer. Of the typologies of democratic transitions mentioned at the beginning of this section, the rarest ones originate in some sort of mobilization of society. The purest example of a democracy born directly out of an armed revolt of democratic forces (Costa Rica's 1948 revolution) is also the only one. What is more likely is that pressures from society, ranging from peaceful mobilization or passive resistance to outright revolt, will provoke responses from the regime that can extend, through nuances, from outright repression to extrication.[21] In the latter case, then, we are back to the strategic context analyzed in the previous paragraphs. That context still includes political actors enmeshed in the old regime. Awareness of the predicament explains some of the prudent conciliatory style with which, in many recent transitions, opponents of the dictatorship have moved in reconstituting an open political community.

My remarks on democratic opposition and civil society apply quite well to transitions from authoritarianism. They apply just as well to the post-totalitarian case. Arguably, in a post-totalitarian regime the chances that the opposition will dispose outright of the regime should be close to nil. This is only in small part, if at all, because organized opposition and civil society are less likely to have survived the totalitarian onslaught. Especially in Eastern Europe, society's resistance to the onslaught and the surprising vitality and extent of what survived are additional proof of totalitarian failure. More important is that extrication will originate in the regime core. Thus, the reforming core will try more earnestly to contain civil society and to co-opt it in support of its own limited *glasnost*. Again, this raises ques-

tions about what it takes to make the reforming core trespass from *glasnost* into democratization, and about the role
of popular opposition in bringing about that shift.

However, the question of who leads transitions from
communism is of relevance at the end of the essay. Here, the
important exercise of comparing contemporary dictatorships has been to highlight that, in turning their crisis in a
democratic direction, prudent conciliation of the old regime
will with few exceptions be required.

But—to add a final twist—conciliation in pursuit of democracy must be reciprocal. We can hardly expect conciliation to be an acquired bias among the opponents of the regime—agreed in principle and implemented accordingly. The
opponents of dictatorship are not a cohesive whole. They
might converge temporarily on the strategies to speed up the
internal crisis of the dictatorship, but there is no reason to
believe that in most cases they will agree instinctively on
how to deal with its orphans. Disagreement is likely to man-
ifest itself precisely when democracy gathers credit as a potential way to resolve the regime crisis. For, at the same time,
a diverse civil society will be gathering greater self-confi-
dence and a more central role, parties will be reconstituted,
barriers to their reconstitution will be lowered, organizations reflecting the various cleavages in society (class, regional, ethnic) will begin agitating, and the season of elections will approach. Conversely, and for good reasons, these
are the same developments that even reformist forces from
the old regime may wish to control. Recent transitions amply support this point. One almost unavoidable aspect of
such developments is the rise of a "left," even a radical left—
a force of extreme opposition to the regime (it could be a
Communist regime)[22], with its own ideas on how to address
the old regime's legacy and on how to replace the dictatorship. What I presented as a challenge to the democratic tran-

sition coming from the old regime has thus become a double challenge. Reconciling the past demands reconciling the future.

In sum, all sorts of coalitions of dissent take shape during a transition. They include the old enemies of the dictatorship, themselves minimally divided on whether their projects are democratic, uncommitted, or clearly nondemocratic. They also include forces seceding from the dictatorship, yet (since secession does not necessarily move toward democracy) similarly divided on their projects. Further, the coalitions compete for the decisive support of a number of uncommitted who, especially in the first stages, may well constitute a majority.[23] The point is to transform these essentially negative, uncertain, shifting, competing, even conflicting coalitions into one coalition of consent for democracy.[24]

To ready ourselves for the analysis of how this can be done, of how Dahl's axiom can be fulfilled, I close the chapter with the issue of democracy's weakness and strength.

DEMOCRACY AS COMPROMISE

The weakness of democracy is its strength. The weakness is one reason why reconstituting a system of coexistence frequently demands careful crafting. The strength is what makes crafting possible.

Democracy's chances to root itself are weak, we are told, because it is a system of compromise, a set of rules for mediating plural and competing interests, to which, in addition, a country takes poorly after the trauma of a dictatorship's collapse. There are echoes, here, of arguments on why some countries cannot afford democracy. Although our aim is to transcend such arguments, there is a kernel of truth to them. We must use this kernel to coax democracy's strength out of its weakness.

In a way, expressions such as "compromise" or "bargain" applied to democracy are misnomers because they may convey a picture of contestants meeting halfway for the purpose of sharing or exchanging spoils and positions that each contestant covets. The resulting compromise is on outcomes, and the outcomes are noncompetitive, fixed, certain, preordained, if not immediate. It is one way of achieving coexistence, but it is not democracy's way.[25] One problem about fixed outcomes: once they become obsolete, as they will over time, there are no rules for renegotiation.

Democracy circumvents the problem because its agreement is not on fixed outcomes but on a competitive political market giving contestants fairly equal chances to affect and share in outcomes. Even better, the agreement is on rules to keep the market competitive. And we are not discussing just democratic theory. As removed as their practices may be from deontology—what they do from what they should do—existing democracies are a reasonable approximation of that political market. A political market is what political actors in a prospective democracy are knowingly called to agree on. Agreement is about uncertainty, as Przeworski calls it;[26] an uncertainty about political outcomes that results from a competitive political market with multiple arenas.[27]

In a nondemocracy outcomes are predictably linked to politico-institutional and/or socioeconomic positions. Privileged social formations or corporate institutions will step in authoritatively if expectations about outcomes are violated. In a democracy, the adoption of a competitive political market tends to circumvent the production of fixed and repetitive outcomes by those positions—winners always winning and losers losing. Institutional dispersion and the removal of politico-institutional monopolies curb institutional sources of certainty. At the same time, by legalizing equal access to institutional positions and by deploying them to countervail

socioeconomic positions, democracy also corrects the un-
equal effects of social and economic privilege. It is in sum
the essence of political democracy that no single social or
institutional formation should determine outcomes by mo-
nopolizing and fusing institutions or by its sheer social position.

As we have proceeded, uncertainty—democracy's weakness—has shaded into its strength. Our choice of words res-
onates the change. Because of the democratic game's very
uncertainty, because it is open and open-ended, and because
none of its players should lose once and for all and on all
arenas, it may finally emerge as attractive, convenient, or
compelling to some detractors—loyalists and enemies of the
old dictatorship alike. The coalitions of dissent from dictatorship mentioned above can converge on one coalition of
consent for democracy that draws strength precisely from
uncertainty; a coalition that can embrace a wide spectrum
of opponents and former loyalists of the dictatorship, ex-
cluding, if unavoidable, only a few weakened dissenters.

At this point of the exposition, it is no longer a puzzle
why any social or institutional formation may prefer the uncertainty of democracy, or, more precisely, why it may consent at times to be a loser. To begin with, consenting to lose
is an axiomatic condition for winning at other times. As
Robert Dahl puts it in *After the Revolution?* consenting to
lose is, if nothing else, a matter of self-interest—no more, no
less. I accept democratic decisions as my own, whether or
not, individually taken, they will benefit me because "I cannot satisfactorily gain my own ends unless I allow others an
opportunity to pursue their ends on an equal basis."[28]
Moreover, accepting this bargain seems to the Dahl of *After
the Revolution?*—singularly different from the author of *Polyarchy*—an almost inescapable event. He depicts the alternatives (isolation, anarchy, despotism itself) as rooted in a

Hobbesian egotism destined sooner or later to crumble. Whether or not despotism is so destined, let us say that, if a crisis strikes, accepting the bargain may make sense not only to the convinced democrat, who needs no demonstration, but also to those who benefited from the certainty of the old despotism and to those among its enemies who may otherwise long to replace it with their own brand of certainty. In the latter two cases, the bargain is acceptable when, with the old certainty in crisis, the bargain's open-endedness seems less costly, more promising, or downright inescapable when compared with preserving that certainty or replacing it with a new one. So we are finally back where we began.

So much for principles. Execution, implementation, getting the job done are always trickier matters that touch directly on crafting, about which I have promised more than I have delivered. It is the subject of the next two chapters.

CHAPTER IV

How Crafting Can Help the Transfer of Loyalties

In all transitions crafting copes with the same problem—the uncertainty of democratic outcomes. The problem (and its treatment) presents, however, varying degrees of difficulty from case to case. Given this uncertainty, given the puzzle of estimating what rewards are promised by the democratic game, the task of democratic transitions is to build what I have called a borrowed, or presumptive, legitimacy. This is done in one way only: by outlining in advance the rules of the game—the norms, procedures, institutions whose operation should effect a fair balance of winning and losing. The outcomes are uncertain; the rules cannot be uncertain. Conflict will remain, but, ideally, there will be no conflict over the rules. For the compromise verges precisely on the rules. The point is one leitmotif of my essay.

Still, what balance will finally emerge? Because rules are not yet operative, actors must guess. Therefore, how much uncertainty is acceptable when guessing? How relaxed will actors be about their guess? This is where cases differ. When

I first spoke of "borrowed" legitimacy, I suggested that the willingness to trust that a fair balance will ultimately eventuate will itself vary. It will vary with political actors and situations. Let me add that it will also vary with the rules that are chosen for the game.

Indeed, democracies differ, at times substantially, in the way they try to balance wins and losses, in the instrumentalities they choose to guarantee political equality, in how they regulate competitive access to government. The instrumentalities are quite concrete, too, once we move from the realm of principles to that of practice and implementation. They have to do with how decision makers are selected and how decisions are taken. They are concerned not only with how (and which) interests are represented but also with how they are aggregated to give decisions legality. Instrumentalities are therefore concerned with relations between democratic institutions. Moreover, one recurring theme in the selection of instruments is balancing the rights of the opposition, and its prospects of winning, against the rights of those who govern. To put it in a slightly different manner, choosing rules that satisfy everybody may easily clash with the political actors' other concern: to obtain rules for political selection that, although competitive, also help one's own side to conquer the government. Alternatively, it may clash with the desire of a minority, which sees its prospects for government as exceedingly dim, to obtain rules that curb majority rights.

In sum, fulfilling Dahl's dictum—that consenting to lose is a condition for winning at other times—encounters some human recalcitrance. The game has no optimal set of rules, that is, no set capable of attracting essential players under most circumstances. But some rules fare better when recalcitrance becomes a serious problem. Adopting such rules—identifying, shaping, and selling them to other political actors—is therefore particularly important in such cases.[1] To put this more forcefully, there are two ways to look at how recalcitrant players affect democratic transitions. One way says that the greater the number and significance of such players, the less likely the transition will be to succeed. The other—in a reversal of the argument to which the reader is now accustomed—says that the more recalcitrant the players, the more the transition will need to seek democratic rules that stress coexistence above everything else.[2] It stands to reason that reluctant players will be more attracted to the democratic game if the representation of their interests in a democratic form is a paramount concern. It stands to reason that if some players worry that their interests will be disregarded or minoritarian, all players, whatever their investment in democracy, may be better served by rules that embrace fair and equal representation. Elsewhere I have called these rules *garantista* rules, or rules of *garantismo*.[3]

We all know that, social science functionalism notwithstanding, just because something is needed or beneficial (such as toleration) does not mean it is forthcoming. On the contrary, something may be in short supply where it is most needed. But this vicious circle is not necessary either. Political actors in a transition are not passive tools of history. If actors are aware of predicaments endemic to transitions and act in their own interests, then they *can* set in motion a process that, even under an unpromising start, may close (be it only in a few cases) with the adoption of appropriate democratic rules.

Before showing how, before returning to *garantismo*, the next section will explain why recalcitrance, and therefore care in crafting the appropriate rules, are especially important in contemporary transitions.

ON THE PREDICAMENTS OF PAST
AND PRESENT TRANSITIONS

If players in the transition were not recalcitrant, then the choice of the appropriate democratic rules would not be a serious problem. In such a case (wherein the players would share an implicit bias for democracy) none of them, by definition, would be facing a dilemma between regime alternatives. Further, sharing a bias for democracy, they would therefore share a readiness to tolerate and trust each other. The two facts obviate the need for a complex and possibly divisive search for explicit and elaborate rules of the game. They mean in particular that no special emphasis on mutual guarantees would be required—such guarantees being implicit and preexisting. They also mean that the uncertainty of the democratic game—the uncertainty of future performance, the prospect of even considerable slack in performance—would not trouble its players to the extent of jeopardizing the transition. They mean finally, and most importantly, that in such transitions the very presence of an implicit trust in the restrained behavior of the other allows players to accept forms of majoritarian democracy and strong party government that in other hands would be suspected of curtailing mutual guarantees. Fear of the tyranny of the majority would not be a stumbling block in drawing the new democratic rules.

This, however, is a largely hypothetical case. It may have been closer to the facts (though I have expressed reservations) when democracy was achieved by the expansion of suffrage in already liberal competitive systems. But the last time this path of democratization was followed was in the aftermath of World War I.[4] Since then, transitions to democracy have been transitions from dictatorial regimes. Let us therefore trace our steps back to my discussion of these crises. I suggested that a transition from dictatorship that does not require coming to terms within the democratic compromise with reluctant nondemocratic players is a rarity indeed. In all likelihood such players will be in abundant supply after a successful domestic revolution, even if the revolution is democratically inspired. There may be fewer if, in a total war, a dictatorship were utterly defeated, and the inviability of the dictatorship's ideology and practice has been unequivocally demonstrated. But we saw that the generalization is based exclusively on the uniquely tragic experience of the defeated Axis powers. I should add that, in my opinion, the Federal Republic of Germany is actually the only former Axis power whose democratic reconstruction fits the generalization comfortably. Only there were authoritarian players confined to a marginal status. Only there was the conversion of authoritarian players to the democratic game not a stumbling block.[5]

The reader remembers, by contrast, the transitions from dictatorship that are most common nowadays. I am abstracting and simplifying, but one can think of a number of fitting cases—especially from Latin America, southern Europe, and Asia. Although still in their infancy, transitions in the Communist world also come to mind. Transitions tend to originate nowadays from the efforts of autocratic governments to extricate themselves. There will be a seceding "right" that, by its efforts at extrication, sets in motion (examples are Greece and Argentina; a prospective one may be Hungary) or accelerates (the Philippines, Poland) a regime crisis. But that right is not quite able or willing to push for full democratization because it is divided over the handling of the crisis, or because it is at odds with the regime's core, or because it is that core. There will be a "left" that, even if sold on democracy (and not all will be), may not be sold yet on *this* democracy. It may fear the reappearance of the past in new guises (what in Spanish is called *continuismo*) or the outright failure of the democratic experiment, and may therefore be vulnerable to the blackmail of its extreme fringes. And there will be a center comprising forces with an implicit bias for democracy or, more simply, with a bias for strategic moderation. The strategic objective of the center is the immediate reconstitution of an open and diverse political community. Its moderating behavior is crucial, though not sufficient, in determining the outcome of the crisis.

Thus, we are not witnessing an overly promising predicament. At the same time, the situation is rather indeterminate. It may be difficult to succeed, but the predicament does not have to close in failure. Notice, for example, how each group of political actors in the transition may be internally divided on strategies and often uncertain about its own interests, how tried and true alliances may dissolve. This makes for an open-ended strategic context. What is involved in that context is not so much accommodating divergent interests—which implies that the interests are firmly defined—as shifting or redefining those interests and their treatment so that political realignments and unorthodox coalitions are possible. Choosing appropriate rules by which democratic politics will represent and process those interests is in fact one way to redefine those interests and point the political process in a democratic direction.

Finally, let us revert to a discussion of how this can be done. I shall employ three scenarios to show how transitions that unfold shakily from our unpromising predicament may still settle on appropriate rules and resolve the predicament (or else may founder). Each scenario starts with one of the three main players in our transitions (a recalcitrant right, a recalcitrant left, or a moderating center) being at least temporarily the pivot of the transition. This may happen because one actor seizes the initiative, or by default because the other two (most fittingly the right and left) prevent each other from seizing it. Because each scenario is abstracted from past, and by now closed, episodes (Italy, Spain, and Portugal in particular), all three are couched in the language and in the referents of transitions from right-wing regimes in the European context. Nevertheless, with suitable adjustments—and with the promise to explore later post-totalitarian and Third World transitions—we can extend some of the lessons to other transitions.

Indeed, the value of the three scenarios is not that they are the most likely ones, but rather that they are exemplary and instructive. They possess an internal plausibility that best illustrates what is fundamentally at issue in turning people toward democracy.[6] The scenarios can be used advantageously to see how to beat the odds against democracy—how to make the improbable possible.[7]

TWO SCENARIOS FOR *GARANTISMO*

The First Scenario

Let us assume the presence of a significant seceding right and an equally significant radical-to-reformist left. Neither is quite convinced by the democratic option, neither is necessarily and uniformly averse to it, and each is checkmating the other. The setting confronts the moderating center squarely with what I have described as the transition's double challenge: reconciling the right (the past) demands reconciling the left (the future, so to speak).[8] The double reconciliation is part and parcel of that reconstitution of the political community, which is the moderating forces' strategic objective. Nonetheless, the moderating forces face two difficulties: the trade-off instinctively sought by the right for agreeing to democracy, and the reaction of the left. Even if, as the scenario assumes, the moderating forces are in control, and even though the right shows signs of relenting, difficulties remain.

The right includes institutions that had central roles in the old regime (especially the military, but possibly also institutions such as the monarchy or the church), which are likely to interpret the democratic bargain in ways that thwart its authentic meaning. As public institutions, used to the certainty of corporate monopolies, their foremost goal in the bargain is not a probable share of future wins and losses (something more appropriate when the allocation of material resources or competitive offices is at stake) but, at least as an opener, the immediate preservation of some of their exclusive institutional roles. Beyond a certain point, similar demands can turn the new regime into a hybrid—a guided democracy of sorts, a political market that tolerates corporate monopolies of institutions and outcomes. Moreover, the point beyond which institutional concerns cease to be legitimate is itself a matter of dispute. Hence the democratic forces may find it difficult to relent on these points, even though they recognize that institutions that served the past regime can also serve democracy. Compounding the difficulties is that those institutions will also expect that any future government will exercise considerable restraint when dealing with their responsibilities under the past regime.

By comparison, it may seem that the right's economic interests are more easily reconcilable to democracy. Productive interests may be accommodated within the allocational logic of wins and losses, and their social bases should be sensitive to the opportunities for democratic representation. Therefore, taken alone, the immediate economic fears of the right (economic downturns tied to the transition, excessive democratic controls over the economy and over traditionally authoritarian labor relations, the rise of a new culture of social demands and participation, and a generally antibusiness climate) more than inducing business to oppose effectively the democratic transition may affect the future performance of the new democracy. But when the fears of business overlap, as they often do, with the weightier reservations held by the state apparatus (with its potential for violence) toward democratic developments, the moderates' task is magnified.

The left's view of the right's concerns and its place in the future political order similarly complicates the task of the center. The scenario assumes that the left (like the right) is sensitive to the need for some national reconciliation and that its most radical fringes—perhaps for tactical reasons if nothing else—are not actively opposed to a democratic outcome. In fact, we can also assume that the left is supporting, even actively pushing for, a democratic outcome (though not *any* democratic outcome).[9] Still, the left may not quite be able to rid itself of the belief that right-wing pressures and the feebleness of the center will expose the new democracy to at least creeping *continuismo*—the inability to shake off the past. The belief is common to practically any transition from dictatorship (and is not necessarily exclusive of the left). But it can become strategically significant when, as in Latin America and the Iberian Peninsula, which gave us *continuismo*, the transition involves extrication. *Continuismo* is then perceived to affect institutions and their culture, as well as the economy and society. It is therefore seen to impede, among other things, a more equitable redistribution of wins and losses for the lower classes. The social criticism and the civic-institutional criticism of the left thus converge to raise skepticism about what the nascent democracy can accomplish and to call for vigilance.

The scenario does not draw distinctions between radicals and reformists within the left, but this is not because there are none. The very labels suggest long-standing differences.

Yet, this scenario raises the clear possibility that the differences will be set aside by a transition climate that allows the radicals to blackmail or attract reformers and to reorient them toward common action. We have here one typical scenario development where normal interests and alliances are redefined and reshuffled by contingencies. And though the reshuffling may be neither permanent nor total (too much may still divide radicals and reformers), two consequences still follow for the center. First, it may still find itself in a position of government (the right may oppose the presence of the left in government, except in a minor or temporary role), but it will be government by default. Second, the center cannot be certain that convergence between radicals and reformists will be less than permanent and full (only a scenario builder, who toys with options, can), nor does it have to. In the short and decisive run, those convergences still sound an alarm for the center's strategic objective.

I have mentioned that the right may object to a government role for the left; but it can object to much more. With the center in a pivotal role and with the two wings recalcitrant yet not opposed to a democratic outcome, the scenario will necessarily unfold to the point where the matter of recognition/reconstitution of political parties and unions is taken up. Here, the right may counter the left's resistance to *continuismo* with demands to constrain its place in the democratic bargain. Its particular concern will be the radical or extreme fringes of the left. Without necessarily pushing for a ban on the extreme left, it may insist on party licensing based on ideological-organizational criteria that the extreme left may not be able to meet; or it may ask for a decoupling of party-union ties, controls on labor unions, and constraints on bargaining powers and job action. The least we can expect is that a left with a strong and potentially hegemonizing radical component may encourage the right to slow

down and restrict democratization. This may include efforts
to delay the electoral process and the reorganization of parties, or to adopt particularly restrictive electoral laws, or to
narrow the agenda of policy reforms. It may also involve
pressures to place the transition in the hands of select party
cartels in which the right will be represented, but from which
more popular forces will be banned, or to assign exclusive
supervisory prerogatives to a special institution of the right
(a military committee, for example). These and similar semi-
democratic arrangements have come to be known by a
Spanish neologism, as *democraduras*.[10]

As with the left, I have drawn no distinctions between
factions of the right, but not because none exist. In the case
of the right, differences become progressively salient as the
old regime breaks down and secession begins. But the scenario raises the clear possibility that those differences are
reabsorbed by a more reluctant nucleus of the seceding right
when choices must be made about new rules of the game.
This nucleus can blackmail or attract sectors of the moderate center itself. Thus, democratization can founder amidst
the postponements I just described, and the reluctance of
right (and left) can turn into a recipe for polarization and
failure if not addressed effectively.[11]

At the same time, everything in the scenario suggests the
implausibility of breaking the impasse by disregarding and
freezing the extremes out of the democratic compromise: it
is risky and, possibly, precipitous. Given the constraints exercised by right and left, the task of the moderating center
might best be to induce the extremes to make reciprocal sacrifices that go beyond original intentions or expectations in
exchange for protecting their ability to coexist in some reformed way. That is the task of institutional *garantismo*.

Taken as the centerpiece of the democratic compromise,
garantismo is an approach to rule making that stresses the

competitiveness of the political market. Its aim is to avoid prejudging or loading the future wins or losses of anyone who abides by the market's intentionally easy rules for admission. The openness and uncertainty of the political market and its outcomes can be achieved in two ways. One way is to ease competitive representation by such measures as electoral proportionalism, a resulting multiparty system, accentuated parliamentarism, concurrent or competitive policy roles for the opposition, an executive with weak legislative initiative and weak programmatic instruments. Another way is to introduce checks and balances, or countervailing powers, functional-institutional (an "activist" constitutional court) or territorial (regionalism) in nature. In these two ways, two monopolies are checked: that of any majority, even temporary, on any institution; that of any institution on outcomes. In sum, under *garantismo* political forces should play in more than one arena, and no single arena or single players are decisive.[12] There follows from all of this that *garantismo* advises against the winner-take-all logic of presidentialism, demanding instead, at the very least, parliamentary democracy. To understand why presidentialism is less likely to offer a safe exit from our scenario is another way of appreciating the advantages of parliamentary democracy—above all if it makes political market competition its centerpiece.[13]

But is *garantismo* likely to be adopted? Can we reasonably fit it into our scenario just because we describe it as needed or beneficial? The reply is that self-interest and awareness—the awareness that *garantismo* is one way to cut the costs of toleration—can help. The adoption of *garantismo* would fulfill Dahl's dictum that in a democracy consenting to lose is a condition for winning; hence it would also fulfill Dahl's further axiom that democracy is more likely once the costs of toleration become lower than those of suppression.[14]

The incentive for the left and right to accept *garantismo* is in the fact that the immediate alternative is a reciprocal stalemate fed by recalcitrance and polarization, with no visible exit. For both left and right, it is therefore a matter of replacing an uncontrollably constrictive political market (if we can call it a market) with an open one. And though the trade-off calls for previously unintended sacrifices, *garantismo* is meant to compensate for them—so much so that in some cases *garantismo*, instead of being proffered by the moderating center, may be solicited by recalcitrant players who finally discover that no other options are immediately available.[15] Moreover, the prospects of a *garantista* setup can help to reshuffle typical interests and alliances. It may for example help sectors of the radical left shelve earlier and riskier aspirations to forms of democracy more to their liking. It may persuade the institutional right to accept a Communist party on the expectation that *garantismo* should tame it. Though state institutions are not direct players in the competitive game, they do have a salient interest that the game, if resumed, be conducted in an orderly manner. Within our scenario, *garantismo* can offer that assurance, whereas other "stronger" democratic setups may not.[16]

The acceptance of *garantismo* does not mean that left and right will stop questioning the final democratic compromise. On the contrary, the compromise's delicate balancing act will make it the object of more exacting, more recurrent, scrutiny. But once *garantismo* is in place, questioning the compromise will also appear less credible and urgent. And this is a reason, special to the moderating center, why that center should support *garantismo*. But there are other and more immediate reasons.

Garantismo should often imply the formation—ad-hoc, formal, or implicit—of broad and inclusive constitutional coalitions, reaching the peripheries of the political spectrum.

It should also discourage the moderate center from committing itself to any institutional choice or policy reform that may be interpreted as leaning toward the left or the right— that is, toward "excessive" or "insufficient" democratization. There are advantages that the center can tease out of these coalitional and policy postures. By holding steadily the middle road, the moderating parties affirm their identity as unquestionably democratic parties, declare their preeminent interest in the peaceful resolution of the transition, and strengthen their pivotal role in that task. In so doing, they can also strengthen and extend their electoral appeal at a time when political alignments are not yet defined. At the same time, though the delicate compromise offered by *garantismo* will be subject to continuous testing and questioning, and announce the advent of a season of disenchantment with democracy's achievements, this should not happen until *garantismo* is put to full use. When it is being adopted, and as the prospect of a democratic exit from the transition becomes more likely, a sense of shared expectations, especially among the left, should be more typical. By helping the right and left to break the impasse, these developments also increase the prestige of the center.

If, in sum, the most reluctant players on both sides may start with an interest in blackmailing and dividing the democratic parties, *garantismo* can subsequently provide incentives across the political spectrum to stem and even reverse that polarizing trend. The scenario starts, after all, from a position of reluctance and circumspection, not of total closure and unconditional opposition. Matters can escalate, but there is no reason why circumspection and suspicion per se should in short sequence close the door to a democratic order. We may as well expect the opposite. The mobilization of large sectors of society that inevitably accompanies the crisis of the dictatorship, the desire for normalization that

follows the initial and often more turbulent period of transition, and the hard reality of painstakingly seeking an exit
from the transition should all work in the same direction,
that of creating a climate in which the prospect of a viable
democratic exit, with all its limits, is favorably received, even
by reluctant actors themselves. It is this climate that should
motivate democratic actors to bolster the case for *garantismo*.[17]

Finally, as signs of possible realignments favoring democracy gather momentum, a point may be passed beyond which
a growing number of political actors who had found it premature to declare themselves for democracy can no longer
afford to stay behind.[18] Thus, our scenario is compatible
with a *garantista* exit, in that the scenario tends toward a
progressive narrowing of the options that are present in the
first stages of the transition, a narrowing in which the democratic parties increasingly play the central role.

The case that inspired the scenario, without fitting it perfectly, is that of Italy. The impression is strong that postwar
Italian democracy is the product of the defeat of fascism and
Allied occupation. But, protected by the Allied shield, domestic political forces played an essential and largely auton-
omous role in replacing fascism and in advancing the democratic reconstruction of the country, even before fascism's
military defeat.[19] Typically, the forces included a right-wing
compromised by having worked till recently with the Fascist
regime and now attempting to rescue itself, a moderate center progressively dominated by the Christian Democratic
party, and a Marxist left dominated at the end of the war
by one of the strongest Communist parties this side of the
Iron Curtain. The emerging *garantista* system—an ostensibly improbable one under the circumstances, yet one that
moved Italian politics out of the impasse and characterizes
it to this day—reflected a difficult, willy-nilly convergence of

the political center and the extreme left to which a more marginal and compromised right had to reconcile itself.

In essence, *garantismo* resulted from the moderating choices of political actors who, barely able to see eye-to-eye, could not discount each other either without imperiling their survival. Moreover, these moderating choices frequently had to be imposed by each set of actors (at the cost of bitter internecine battles) on reluctant fellow actors. Thus, as the Fascist government was overthrown and civil war began, it was the top leadership of the Communist party that convinced its cadres and other political parties to form a wartime national unity government that included a monarchical right compromised by fascism. And it was the Christian Democratic party, soon to emerge as the dominant force in the government, that kept the difficult understanding with the left afloat during war and reconstruction. To be sure, cooperation was strained, marred by reciprocal suspicion, employed to buttress one's own positions, and meant to last until the time when the Christian Democrats and the left would naturally and safely oppose each other.

But that time never really came. Thus, as the cold war escalated, and the Marxist left was definitively expelled from the unity government, the move was accompanied, to make it infinitely more palatable, by the collective formulation and nearly unanimous adoption of the most strongly *garantista* constitution issued by a postwar democracy. In fact, as the prospects of its political isolation became clearer, the left increasingly turned toward *garantismo* as a cherished tenet and a constitutional capstone. Because of this arrangement, a permanent opposition could hold accountable and influence centrist governments for years to come. At the same time, the Christian Democratic party's ability to avoid, through *garantismo,* both a showdown with and a surrender to the left—its ability to hold the political center while resisting the appeals of the right—must be seen as crucial in its emergence as the recognized bulwark of young Italian democracy. The party still dominates Italian governments.

Finally, if *garantismo* was possible in the 1940s—when the continuing confrontation between authoritarian and democratic worldviews did not make it natural—its prospects appear better nowadays, when worldviews about democracy versus dictatorship have substantially changed. They also appear better in light of the greater regard that, out of self-interest, left and right demonstrate for the value of mutual accommodations. On one side, more room exists for a left that, without ignoring the risk of backlashes from the right, appreciates the ability of a reformed right to operate in a democracy. It is a left confident that, by reacting with greater caution to the right, it does not automatically sell out its own future role. It is a left that could subscribe to the words of a member of the executive committee of Spain's Socialist party: "Democracy and its consolidation come first, before our political programmes . . . because the Spanish right has shown that it can live very well under both authoritarian and democratic regimes, while the left can only survive within a democratic framework."[20] It is a left that, even if wary of initiating an institutional compromise with the right, may be open to compromise because of attraction, convenience, or compulsion.

On the other side, the right has reason to shed its reluctance because of the universal discredit befalling authoritarianism and the high normative standards attached more recently to democracy as a means to recreate a political community. The postponements and niggardly accommodations promised by a *democradura* can hardly compete with participation, representation, equality, popular accountability, and the other standards of democracy to which contemporary public opinion seems ever more alert and which *gar-*

antismo best embodies. A right that stops short of full political democracy risks the rapid waning of any credibility its political formula may have. In sum, no extrication, no exit. *Garantismo* thus stands out as a better option for the right as well.

But, with the last remarks, we are now shading into the second scenario. It too starts in an apparently unpromising way yet finds a democratic exit. And here too *garantismo* seems to offer an institutional solution that political actors should find convenient to embrace.

The Second Scenario

The second scenario unfolds with the seceding right in control. Is it a promising start, or is it not? Consider the following course of events. Imagine that signs of an impending dictatorship crisis are still muted. For the purpose of forestalling a crisis with no exit, a seceding right initiates a partial liberalization of the regime and therefore distances itself from its more committed leaders and supporters. Imagine that this is done in anticipation of more forceful moves by the democrats in an effort to bend them to one's own game. In itself, this constitutes the beginning of a crisis. The secessionists hope, however, it will be a "guided" one that will stop where the secessionists want. Yet, as we see from the closing remarks of the first scenario, a secession that takes the route of liberalization may not stop there.

It is one thing to secede and be ahead of the other political forces, but another to guide the whole transition alone. Sooner or later, as in the first scenario, pressures for greater political innovation and for broader or different coalitions for change will be brought to bear by newly mobilized groups. These forces will regard the dictatorship as morally abhorrent, economically inviable, politically exhausted, internationally isolated, or plainly expendable. The resentful views will surface precisely because a secession is under way. For a seceding right to resist those pressures and views, to stop short of full political democracy after having distanced itself from the old regime, would be to alienate the democrats and the newly mobilized forces in general—perhaps more so or with greater costs than in the first scenario.

Also, the right is not in the best position to disregard these newly mobilized forces. By taking action to change the regime, the secessionists have already alienated its hard core. They may therefore find it difficult either to convert or to control and overpower that core, unless they seek wider support on their left—among the democrats and, in general, among the dictatorship's more reasonable enemies. If instead, discouraged or unconvinced, the secessionists try to retrench from liberalization and return to the fold, they may bring discredit and worse on themselves. A seceding right commits treason much more clearly than in the first scenario, where the initiative belonged to the moderating center. Its return to the fold, after defecting and losing, may prove unfeasible.

So, let us assume that the seceding right turns instead toward the democrats, indeed toward the left. But the democrats' support should exact a price. Since they are not natural allies of the right, they have good reasons to suspect its motives and commitment. Obtaining their support may therefore require deeds that explicitly and progressively demonstrate the right's commitment. Some of the most obvious deeds, and possibly the easiest, are politico-institutional: simply permitting forces that play by the rules to enter the political market while avoiding institutional arrangements that appear to stack outcomes in favor of a reformed right. Such deeds sound very much like *garantismo*. Thus the scenario ends with a conversion of the seceding right—or a decisive fraction of it, which then secedes in turn. The conversion is not only to political democracy but also to a particularly open brand of it.

I wish to add that in this scenario the *garantista* solution can achieve a safer legitimation of the new order than in the first one. First, *garantismo* initiated by the right may be accepted as a more complete antidote against the residues of the past. Second, by allaying, if not removing, some of the concerns about the residues of the past, the right may convince the democrats and the left to push for fewer reforms of the civil, political, and military apparatus of the old state. This is the more likely if, as it moves toward democracy, the seceding right can maintain its advantage over the other reform forces, anticipate their moves, and set the agenda of democratic reconstruction. Third, in the hands of the right *garantismo* should simultaneously be offering the more reluctant sectors of the old regime—possibly the military or the party apparatus—greater assurance of an orderly, not excessively "ambitious," transition. One important factor in reconciling to democracy the most reluctant members of the old guard is the expectation that the right, by mastering the transition, will also dominate party and government politics in the first crucial years, thus providing stability.

In sum, the second scenario suggests that a democratic transition for which a seceding right can take much of the credit may offer a stronger base of consent. It allows what I have called elsewhere a mutual "backward-forward" legitimation of the enemies of the dictatorship, on the one hand, and of reformed forces formerly in the service of the dictatorship, on the other.[21] This convergence may take the shape of a formal or informal constitutional coalition, working on the rules of the game and stretching to embrace even forces that, although conventionally labeled extremes, may find important payoffs in the collective implementation of *garantismo*. Also, the ability of *garantismo* to effect a stable transfer of loyalties may be such that, with the transition over, it no longer needs to be the constitutional centerpiece. Such democratic practices as majority rule, party government, and executive privilege may gain ground without stirring feelings that the rules have been illegitimately changed to the detriment of any force that put its trust in *garantismo*.[22] *Garantismo* shall have exhausted its function.

In concluding this discussion of the second scenario, I wish to emphasize that the scenario starts from, but also makes sense of, the assumption that the right is committed to the past not by ingrained nostalgia but by the structure of opportunities. To argue that secessions serve the purpose of saving old interests (*plus ça change . . .*) begs the question of how such a goal can be achieved. Desires and intentions are somewhat beside the point. Strictly speaking, saving old interests through creating a new regime is an impossibility because the rules of a regime affect and hence define/redefine the interests served. And if this sounds like an overstatement, it is still true that in a democracy the prospects of somehow preserving, even in part, old interests are or appear uncertain. To be sure, that is why secessionists may wish to stop the process of liberalization before the threshold of democracy. But there are circumstances, as in our scenario, where holding back may no longer make sense.

As anticipated, one country above all—Spain—has inspired the scenario. It is no coincidence that I first spoke of "backward-forward" legitimation in a paper comparing the Spanish transition with transitions in southern Europe. Spain best illustrates the internal plausibility of the scenario.[23] When Francisco Franco died, the regime was not exactly in crisis. Nevertheless, the remarkable social growth of the country, its Europeanization, the revival of civil society, the emergence of more or less loyal oppositions—all changes occurring in the later Franco years—were signals of regime obsolescence, even as the regime could take credit for some of them. Following Franco's death, liberalization at the hand of civilian sectors of the regime (governmental, political, economic, bureaucratic) was typically meant to forestall crisis. But in the space of seven months, bolder representatives of the regime overtook the liberalizers to effect a sharper regime break. It was the clearest example perhaps of an authoritarian regime that abolishes itself for good. The move toward democracy was accompanied by a *política de consenso* embracing vast sectors of the democratic center and the left, as well as by a progressive, if never guaranteed, acceptance of the transition by the regime's institutional hard core (the military in particular). *Consenso* was obtained by strict cooperation in forming the rules of the game. The rules therefore came to emphasize the openness of the political game and the ability of political actors to play in different arenas, including the regional ones. At the same time, the secessionists maintained their control of the consensual process and of the government, reaping electoral victories through the transition.[24] The central role played by the secessionists, combined with their opening to other political forces, made of the Spanish transition both a *reforma* and *ruptura pactada*.[25]

In closing, I must point out that although the second scenario is typical of an authoritarian crisis in a Western context, it and the specific example of Spain became attractive in the late 1980s to regime reformers and opponents alike in some Eastern European countries. The reminder will suffice for the time being.

ONE SCENARIO AGAINST *GARANTISMO*

The Third Scenario

This last scenario shall illustrate, by the costs of its absence, why *garantismo* can be a convenient exit for reluctant players. I have said in the first scenario that the left, including what we conventionally label a radical left, is nowadays more likely to understand the importance of making accommodations with the right. And if it is not? Our optimism, after all, should not be excessive.

The left usually operates in a context of extrication, so it is often but one of a number of players at best. This explains in good part the left's greater understanding of the need for accommodation. But let us suppose that the left, in fact some radical brand of it, turns out to dominate other players in the first stages of the transition. Let us further suppose that the radical left is a leading force in bringing the crisis of the dictatorship to a head through, for instance, a successful plan of civil mobilization and disobedience. There is in fact a very interesting and unusual case (Portugal) in which regime extrication and radical mobilization combined almost symbiotically. If the left is initially in control, it is not difficult to imagine a scenario in which the left pushes at least for a "progressive" democracy, one that would not be confined to its political shell but would place institutional and class relations on a more "advanced" basis and liquidate all residues of the old regime. Radicals would follow such a route for many reasons.

Their unique position (radicals do not win every day) may give them additional confidence and inspire them to unique ambitions. It may impress them with a sense of potentially expanding authority and support and hence with a conviction that much is possible, or that much could be attempted before it is too late. The fear of backlashes, which in the other scenarios induces the radical left to more restrained behavior, here may induce it to exploit its advantage. After all, if radicals find themselves in the lead, they are there, their thinking goes, because the right (and perhaps not just the right) is morally, politically, and economically bankrupt, and action should and can be taken before it recovers. In general, most transitions to democracy, while compelling a seceding right to prove its case, place the left in the position to claim moral and cultural-political superiority. But feelings of superiority are particularly strong in our scenario. Be it because the radicals feel and act superior, or because they are strategically able to blackmail more moderate sectors of the left, the latter may themselves be drawn in by the prospects of a radical democratization and may therefore opt for or be propelled into coalitions with the radicals.

Let us assume that the left's initial moves catch the right in disarray. What should follow is a process that—even barring options that go clearly past democracy—rapidly and deliberately aims beyond the minimal, noninvasive, strictly procedural reforms best embodied by *garantismo*. The aim is to build a democracy with a strong adjective. Let me suggest three plausible components of this project.

First, we may expect that reforms will tend to give priority to policy content. Ambitious reform policies will seek to prevent a resurgence of the past by attacking those institutions and social relations that the left deems to be the carryovers from the old regime. By producing (or seeming to produce) immediate and tangible results—for instance, revoking a particularly hated institutional privilege, introducing new agrarian relations—the policies will likely garner quick popular consent. Thus, a victorious left may superimpose, as somewhat odd bedfellows, voluntarism (the belief that radical reforms are possible and effective) on determinism (the belief that political relations are the product of ingrained institutional and social relations, which people cannot escape). Because the traditional classes and institutions are bound to resist advanced political relations, they must therefore (and they can) be radically altered or removed.

Second, to protect themselves against backlashes, radicals

will tend to soft-pedal a conventionally competitive constitutional framework—one that emphasizes the uncertainty of
future political outcomes—in favor of politico-institutional
arrangements intended to maintain, monitor, and carry forward radical reforms. Initially, being enticed by populist
democratic utopias, the project may be tempted to experiment with grass-roots forms of monitoring and guidance.
Workers' committees, producers' self-management, people's
councils, and so forth—locally rooted and controlled—may
try to replace or supervise and restrain elected parliaments
and the institutions of the old state. But because these dispersed arrangements are slippery and cumbersome, the left
may very well push toward more effectively centralized forms
of guidance; that is, a peak military or party junta that, as
a guardian of the democratic revolution, assumes veto or
monitoring powers over electoral, parliamentary, constitutional, and reform matters.

Third, a left in pursuit of radical reform policies and
institutional guidance is likely to shun political and constitutional coalitions that share power with more moderate
sectors of the party spectrum as tactically unnecessary, pro-
grammatically stifling, and ideologically improper. It will
prefer to go it alone, or to compel other forces, lest they be
branded disloyal, to join coalitions of national salvation as
dutifully subordinate partners. This contrasts with *garantismo*, where the search for rules of mutual survival mini-
mizes in the long run losses on all sides and naturally calls
for wide-open constitutional and, possibly, government coalitions.

Assuredly, some of the policy and institutional components of the project can also be found in parliamentary democracies with strong party government (as some old democracies are). I am thinking of the emphasis on policy
effectiveness, the homogeneity of the governing forces se-

lecting policies, the constitutional and actual guidance exercised by those forces over representative institutions. But in our scenario, the left is likely to employ those policy and institutional mechanisms, or to surround them with other and more questionable ones (self-appointed juntas with veto powers, for example), in ways that violate democratic restraints. The left may not look at the constitutional mechanisms it has assembled as things to be used interchangeably by its adversaries, were they to become the government. It may not see party government as government by parts, and limited in time. It may not take favorably to uncertainty in institutional outcomes. The purpose of reforms, of juntas and other self-appointed guardians, of innovating with the conventional institutional trappings of democracy is to remove that uncertainty. Minimally, even if the left settles for a more conventional democratic framework that in principle permits a new majority to run the government, it will not consider that majority as being entitled to repeal or alter its reforms, since they define and legitimize the new order.

Yet the problem with letting the reforms of the left define the new order is that they are likely to remain one-sided. In fact, they become divisive. Thus, the left's ambitious reform project, being perverted at first, comes dangerously close to being frustrated in the end. The reforms shall have been introduced, by a select majority if any, to stifle traditional interests in a way that those interests may find intolerable. Most prominent among those interests are those of the state apparatus to manage itself and of capitalism to accumulate. Hence, especially if the left allows some reasonable facsimile of a democratic game to develop (if, for instance, it allows political parties some freedom to organize and to run for office),[26] it is unlikely, *pace* the left's voluntarism, that its reforms will obtain either the effective removal or the sufficient compliance of traditional interests. In fact, the reforms may alarm and awaken those interests, making the belief that the interests cannot adapt a self-fulfilling prophecy. In sum, the same right that under the former scenario was concerned with remedying its deficit of democratic credentials may in this third scenario rally not just against new policies but against the new regime.

But there is more. The left's policies of radical reform, but especially its constraints (in part practiced, in part intimated or feared) on openly competitive politics, will also alienate the moderating center. Though the center may remain aloof from the right, it will nonetheless resent the left's strategy on two grounds: (1) it violates the center's preference for noninvasive strategies, and (2) it violates policy interests—in capitalist accumulation, for example—that the center may share with the right. Thus, a situation of dual power or dual legitimacy should develop between the left in government and the opposition in parliament, between parties and juntas, between the electoral arena and the arena fabricated by self-anointed interpreters of the popular will.

At this point the scenario can take several more or less plausible directions. Hopes of a democratic evolution may collapse either because of a backlash or because the left, confirmed in its resolve by general hostility, removes all vestiges of competitive politics. Alternatively, the duality of power and legitimacy may continue under a more competitive democratic framework. For example, the right may not be able to bear the costs of a countercoup and, ironically, begins to agitate against the suppression of parliamentary rights. At the same time, the left may now conclude from widespread hostility the different lesson that its strategy is counterproductive and retrench. Or it may suffer a setback that further cools its aspirations. The moderates would gain. Even so, left, moderates, and right will continue to compete on issues that touch on the very identity, and therefore the legitimacy, of the new order.

In sum, the scenario serves to illustrate the point that players who are reluctant to trust an open political game, preferring instead to protect themselves against their adversaries by girding democracy with their own invasive measures, may end up with a troubled democracy or worse. If it is a democracy, it should be one in which toleration is still too costly. Would this begin a vicious circle, leading to collapse in any event? We should not claim this much. As with the other scenarios, I shall discuss democratic life after the transition in later chapters.

Let us see the ways in which Portugal fits the scenario. Portuguese democracy, troubled for a number of years, arrived at the predicament from interesting and unusual origins that combined regime extrication and radical mobilization. At the beginning of the 1970s, following Antonio Salazar's incapacitation, Portugal embarked on a timid process of liberalization that was soon stifled by the political toll of colonial warfare in Portuguese Africa. More often than not, any effort at liberalization under such circumstances meets the resistance of the state apparatus, particularly the military. More often than not, a military carrying the burden of colonial or guerrilla warfare will cloak the dictatorship with the new armor of counterinsurgency ideologies. Not so in Portugal.

In Portugal the military finally overthrew the dictatorship. And within the military, officers who had embraced the Third World radicalism of the insurgents soon had the upper hand over officers whose plans seemed to waver between a *democradura* and a cautious political democracy. Thus—a rare occurrence in a case of extrication—the radical left (including early on the Communist party) set itself as the apparent guide of the transition, seeking to construct a tutelary democracy in which populism, Mediterranean socialism, and other ideal ingredients were tentatively mixed in a recipe of difficult execution. But the radical project came to an end in the space of approximately two years, not without leaving, however, a significant legacy of constitutional and policy issues for the more straightforward democracy that finally emerged. Removing or rectifying the legacy of the transition has been one central and difficult task of Portuguese democracy until recently; it is a task that touches upon democracy's institutional legitimacy.

The radical project came to an end because it met with the unexpected, obstinate, and successful resistance not so much from a right in disarray as from a whole spectrum of democratic forces, foremost among them the Socialist party. The resistance pitted parties and parliament against tutelary juntas and revolutionary councils. Why the resistance? Because the democratic parties upheld a view of legitimation that seriously clashed with that of the radical left. In essence, they held what I have presented throughout this essay as the democratically correct and effective view: legitimation must come from shared institutional guarantees for competitiveness before coming from anything else. It cannot come exclusively from securing specific, substantive, and radical reforms. The view of the left—especially because it was in contraposition to, rather than in combination with, the view of the parties—was instead democratically counterproductive. It sought popular legitimation by means of certain, immediate, and substantive reforms (nationalizations, land distribution, decolonization, defascistization). But substantive reforms alone could neither define nor secure democracy. Quite to the contrary, thinking of democracy as a set of substantive achievements led to experimenting with forms of guidance that proved extraneous to democracy. Thus the radical left ended by equating legitimation with its own steady hegemony not just over the transition but also over the future political order; not just over substantive reforms but also in drafting and monitoring the new constitutional system. In so doing, it questioned the legitimacy of the other parties and any other force that might take issue with its special project.

The tug of war between democratic parties and the military—and also within the military—might have ended with the victory of the radicals at the expense of democracy. It ended with their defeat. The defeat of the radical left in Portugal must be linked to their unwillingness to risk mutual tolerance and hence to consider rules of the game that would mitigate the probable costs of tolerance.[27]

CONCLUSIONS

My interpretation of the Portuguese events should sound familiar to the reader of chapter 2, where I referred in a similar vein to the crisis of the second Spanish republic in the 1930s. The reference was used to make the point that contemporary political actors have learned from previous mistakes, such as those committed in Spain. In Portugal, it seems, they had not. In Portugal, as in earlier Spain, there were still political actors who—either because they recognized correctly but with disappointment that democracy is not a tool of coveted social upheaval, or because, on the contrary, they still believed in democracy as a majoritarian lever for willful social progress—showed impatience with the actual give-and-take of the democratic method and, for that matter, of regime transitions.

It would be less than intuitive for actors such as these to renounce their daring quest for immediate results in favor of the still distant and impalpable advantages of democratic

tolerance. Something more and more immediate is needed
to convince or cajole them, if cajoling them is at all still
possible. Signals (events, actions) are needed early on to show
that democratization is moving ahead with speed and delib-
eration, bringing visible benefits for all actors who wish to
concur in the process. Fortunately, side by side with what
Albert Hirschman calls *la rage de vouloir conclure* of would-
be comprehensive social reformers, there exists the other and
more expedient impatience of many who place instead their
first trust in the political and democratic outcome of transitions. It is an impatience with lingering transitions, a desire
to leave their limbo, a hankering to bring the process to a
successful close. If these democrats can put their impatience
to effective use—if they can quickly secure the definition and
implementation of the democratic game and carve out with
sufficient realism the place and resources of its significant
players—then they will be in a better position to turn around
equally impatient comprehensive reformers.

It may be objected that there are actors (the secessionists
and the nostalgics of the old regime in general) who prefer
procrastination and are wary of impatience, and that they
may at times be in charge. Unquestionably, this is a serious
problem, but it is not an insurmountable one. We know that
the motive to procrastinate is not always the unwillingness
to renounce dictatorship but rather the fear that mounting
events will overtake the old interests after all and leave them
without a significant voice in a new order. If signals, contex-
tual to the transition, anticipate that secession from dictatorship to democracy pays, there may be no reason to slow
down, dangerously so, the process. Instead, the signals can
give secessionists, who sense that procrastination jeopardizes their credibility, the needed spur to greater and more
expeditious innovations. The difficult twist is that the signals to reassure secessionists may have to come from would-

be comprehensive reformers as much as from impatient democrats. This is another way of discovering the importance of shared sacrifices.

But these are topics more related to the tactics of transitions. They are topics for the next chapter.

CHAPTER V

Tactics
On How to Sell One's Craft

The rules for guiding future democratic behavior are not chosen in a vacuum. Signals in a transition abound; in fact, there are so many that they get mixed, or they let the last one prevail briefly. Therefore, some signals—those that would make the choice of democratic rules worthwhile—must be made to flash more clearly. There are signals of evanescent, difficult-to-interpret qualities, such as declarations, promises, opinions, styles and demeanor, choices of words, dress, place, and circumstances. I will dispense with discussing them. Other signals are more concrete and precise and involve specific decisions, allocations, behaviors, as well as timing, a quality whose importance is never sufficiently stressed. Timing is important to all actors. I shall argue that an expeditious transition, where signals of material importance to political actors are communicated early (where, in sum, decisions and actions are prompt and reasonably linked), can often prove decisive in fostering acceptance of the democratic game.

Different actors, however, pay attention to somewhat different signals. Mass political actors on one side and state/institutional or economic/functional actors on the other constitute one such example. The latter actors can be grouped in three categories. One comprises the state institutions that ran or served the dictatorship (the military and the single party above all) and whose recycling is at issue. Another is labor, whose consent to the accommodation of the other two categories seems crucial but demands a trade-off. The third (if the transition occurs in the national/international context of capitalist economies) is the economic bourgeoisie, whose interest that the new democracy will not purposely hamper the reproduction of capital requires accommodation. Mass political actors are more directly sensitive to signals of an explicitly political nature (those having to do with expediting free elections above all). Functional and institutional actors are not insensitive to political signals, including those pertaining to their own political representation. Yet as reconstruction impends, they evidently evaluate them in the light of signals that affect their corporate and professional interests more directly. To exemplify the contrast: the political left is more likely, on the one hand, to play along with secessionists if they either call for or accept early elections. On the other hand, the military's readiness to appreciate the stabilizing effects of early elections depends on the willingness of democrats and social reformers to recognize, at a minimum, the vital interests of the military as an impersonal nonpolitical institution.

As the example of the military implies, the distinction between mass political actors and other actors does not hold perfectly. Actors can wear two hats and be sensitive to political as well as functional/institutional decisions. Another, perhaps the best, example is that of labor. It can be sensitive to the reestablishment of democratic life as well as to socioeconomic reforms. Thus, democratic transitions must balance mass political and functional/institutional demands. But how?

I shall argue in this chapter something that, in view of our treatment of the Portuguese case, should come as no surprise: to wit, because of the almost inescapable presence of nostalgics and secessionists in contemporary transitions and because their functional/institutional interests require a corporate identity, reforms in the economy or the state become very difficult to expedite. This may feed disenchantment among popular sectors of regime opposition, which attach great importance to those reforms. But the disenchantment may be alleviated by expeditiously strengthening the features of mass and competitive politics. Hence this chapter places special emphasis on political tactics to this effect—the kind of well-timed tactics and signals for selling democracy that were employed in the Spanish case. The chapter should lend additional support to the thesis that most contemporary transitions demand as a price for their success, especially in the beginning, sacrifices in some areas that are compensated by boldness in others.

These remarks apply quite well to transitions from right-wing authoritarian regimes. They demand adjustments, however, before they can be applied to post-totalitarian systems, where, plainly, reforms to accelerate political democratization cannot be used to offset the lack of other reforms. The reason is that, beyond a certain point, the political democratization of Communist systems cannot proceed without the other reforms. Democracy may be able to operate, and even to allay disenchantment, in a socially imperfect capitalist system. Indeed, keeping the system imperfect may be a temporary trade-off. But democracy cannot operate in a collective economy. It is not a conceivable trade-off. Only in the context of a liberalizing economy that frees political potentials and permits political gains can a reemerging labor movement be asked to make sacrifices like those required by and recompensed in other transitions. But liberalizing a collective economy runs into obstacles. The very choice of economic liberalization brings the need for economic sacrifices—unpalatable and, for most, difficult to make. Liberalization also demands reforming and in large part dismantling party-bureaucratic apparats whose institutional interests are closely connected with the operation of collective economies. Nonetheless, some post-totalitarian systems have made less timid progress than others, and have done so without meeting the ostensibly insurmountable antagonism of the state apparats. The post-totalitarian conundrum will receive more attention toward the end of this chapter.

Much of what I said about the importance of early signals can be pared down to a simple assertion; that is, if you wish to set up an attractive democratic game, do not delay. The proof of the pudding, especially for those who have not yet developed a taste for it, is in the eating. The assertion has some critical implications for the use of pacts between the old regime and the opposition as tools for managing the transition. Pacts may be advisable and even necessary on some matters (most clearly those touching on functional and institutional interests). But is it advisable and necessary to extend them so as to incorporate political constraints (who participates, how soon, and how?) that would make the political game safer for some players? Such tactics may alienate an already reluctant left, in addition to democrats. They would freeze efficient resources, which are perhaps the only ones the regime opposition can rely on as its own.

But these assertions need to be justified in the face of some ostensibly sensible notions; for example, that democracy (like overeating for the starving) requires habituation, or that pressing through the transition can alienate many.

TIME AS A TACTICAL RESOURCE

Regime opponents have good reasons to wish for a speedy transition. And frequently so do secessionists and, for that matter, unreconstructed nostalgics. The transition government is by definition a transitional, indeed provisional, government, falling, so to speak, between legitimacies. Whether a new government is assembled by the opposition or some extension of the old regime, a transition government takes power, as Juan Linz observes, with a specific and temporary mandate: to bring the transition to a close.[1] Assuming generously that the government and its mandate are generally viewed with favor, this favorable attitude is most unlikely to outlive a failure in executing the mandate. Nor can the government circumvent the predicament by neglecting to set up an agenda and a timetable, and appealing instead to the transition's unavoidable imponderables. A government tempted by failure to stretch its mandate into an open-ended or rescheduled future may soon lose credibility. Falling between legitimacies, and faltering, it can draw authority neither from the past regime nor from democratic elections. If the government is made up of secessionists, they will be at odds with unreconstructed nostalgics; if it is put together by regime opponents, it will precede legitimizing elections.

Thus, if the objective is a democratic transition, clear signals that the transition is being implemented—namely, a firm and speedy timetable of mass political reforms—would add credibility to a provisional government. It would also create conditions of greater mutual trust that would eventually alleviate recalcitrance caused by the uncertainty of the incipient democratic game. The most significant signal in that timetable is very likely the calling of free elections.

True, elections do not necessarily bring about democracy. They can be used for ulterior motives; they can be boycotted. It can be said, for instance, that other, more explicit signals should be sent out before calling for freely contested elections. It can be said further that, in the absence of such signals, elections are of dubious effectiveness and purpose. Elections before liberalization—for example, elections before civil liberties, habeas corpus, curbs on state or oppositional violence, and a restored legal order—can be called to take advantage of a temporarily disorganized opposition. This suggests that elections should not be held until liberalization is in effect and that, therefore, prompt democratic reforms are not always possible or advisable. The suggestion is sensible, provided it is not used to justify slowing down liberalization. A slowdown would cause a loss of confidence among regime opponents (even if they happen to run the provisional government) greater than if elections had been called prematurely. For one thing, though liberalization may strike in some ways as more fundamental than elections, taken alone it does not constitute a sufficient signal that a transitional government stands ready to move toward full democratization. On this score—as even the semicompetitive elections held in Poland in 1989 testify—elections are still the least ambiguous signal in addition to being virtually necessary.[2] In other words, if the signal fails (we may think, as a case in point, of Central America), little else is left.

A speedy democratization seems in fact more than ever advisable when the transitional government is run by secessionists. In view of the known and special problems that secessionists have with lending credibility to their transitional plans, the case needs no lengthy restatement. In order to deal with the skepticism that surrounds their plans, secessionist governments often appeal to the advice and consultation of independent groups and individuals, who function as interpreters of the emerging civil society. They constitute drafting and consulting committees with claims to impartiality. They impanel judicial bodies. All these measures, and liberalization in general, may alleviate, but not erase, some of that skepticism. On the contrary, hiding behind those measures to preach a gradual progress toward democracy, while postponing elections to some unknown, riper time, may well prove counterproductive.[3] For, whether a secessionist government recognizes it or not, liberalization mentally evokes democratization, and democratization is signaled by elections.[4] Therefore, liberalization without democratization only raises expectations and rekindles impatience.[5]

Transitions that place elections in a distant, possibly indeterminate, future, or surround them with restrictions and controls, are at times successful. Larry Diamond (whom I just cited in n. 5) mentions Brazil, Nigeria, Thailand, and Indonesia as countries where national elections either have been scheduled deliberately late or (the latter two cases) coexist with an executive still controlled by the military. One may add Taiwan, and Turkey in some ways, as countries at various stages of political change that is both deliberately slow and reined in by the old regime. A few months ago we may have added Hungary and Poland to the list, but their slow pace is already giving way to more daring and perhaps necessary impatience.

The point is that, in all these cases, slowness is not a virtue: it does not reflect some inherently superior and general understanding of how democratization is best pursued. It is a contingent response, prudent at best, to a real *or perceived* necessity. By and large, this necessity hides the unwillingness of secessionists, fearing backlashes or chaos, to surrender power fully. Even in Eastern Europe, where the search for a consensual exit seems to be the most determined one conducted since Spain, a speedier transition is prevented not by some lofty regime commitment to the virtues of democratic gradualism but by the tightly constructed post-totalitarian

Communist regimes themselves. Besides, slowness, even when accepted, has its costs. In Brazil, often cited as a successful example of democratization without full-fledged preliminary elections and under deliberate regime supervision, the slow pace of liberalization had protracted a pattern of elitist, often autocratic, local politics and constrained the already difficult emergence of a mass party system.[6]

Let us now assume that the transitional government is manned not by the old regime but by its opponents. Can the latter dispense with the early signals of democratization that the former so needs? This is hardly the case, despite the greater initial credit that regime opponents may seem to enjoy. We must not forget that a government of regime opponents must cope with constituencies of the old regime, that these constituencies fear that they will be substantially shortchanged in the democratic bargain, and that, paradoxically, this fear may lead them to agitate for their own democratic rights. Equally, we must not forget that if the opponents that run the government are moderates, they must cope with the impatience of comprehensive reformers who, while riding free, may distrust the moderates' ability to resist the constituencies of the old regime. And if the government is run by would-be comprehensive reformers, it may meet with the moderates' resistance to being dragged into substantive reforms by a government that underplays mutual guarantees.

Therefore, not unlike secessionist governments, governments headed by regime opponents should have a clear interest in sending out early signals of democratic intent. The signals serve to reabsorb and tame opposition. Far from plunging a transition into political chaos by being premature, early signals may introduce a measure of order by increasing everybody's stakes in an organized political game. For example, the calling of elections should have the effect of focusing the energies of political actors on the task of winning seats—a specific task with specific returns. Energies previously devoted by the opposition to agitation, without clear rules and stakes, could now be turned to the more constructive business of building electoral machineries and broad winning coalitions.

It is true that transitional governments may be insensitive to the benefits of democratization. Especially for governments by secessionists or comprehensive reformers, democratization may significantly alter their starting goals. Nevertheless, acting in disregard of those benefits has at times irremediable costs and risks. One good example—not because the costs were irremediable, but because it involved a transitional government whose democratic objectives were actually not in question—is the transition in the Philippines. President Corazon Aquino's failure to call for early elections and a constitutional process entrusted to a nonelected provisional body with dubious credentials were significant drawbacks of the democratization process, on which left and right capitalized. A similar lesson can be drawn from the Portuguese transition. In Portugal, free elections and constitution making took place early on. Yet their effectiveness as signals was marred, with serious consequences for the transition and for the radical military that first guided it, by three contradictory signals issued by the radical military: (1) its stifling control over the government and its democratic partners in the government, (2) its dismissal of the elections as pseudodemocratic bourgeois exercises, and (3) its guidance of the constitutional process.

As for the (still limited) electoral experiments under way in Poland, Hungary, and the Soviet Union under the guidance of reforming regimes, there are two ways to look at them. One is to argue that given the socioeconomic crisis and ethnic tensions in these countries and given the added tensions and popular sacrifices necessitated by reforms bearing on these problems, elections (lifting the lid) will increase political chaos. The other way is to argue that, without genuine elections, reforming governments may not be able to justify their calls for sacrifice. Hence elections can curb chaos. More to the point, in post-totalitarian systems elections are inescapable if other reforms must proceed and if reforming governments are serious about their reforms and are willing to face the consequences. The premise is still open to later investigation, but if we take it as demonstrated, its consequences are not.

Indeed, there is another, in some ways more poignant, indication of the power of elections. Even when variously thwarted, confined, manipulated, or just not in the cards, once they are called, elections can still energize and possibly protect democratization beyond the hopes or fears, and indeed beyond the understanding, of the principal actors.

In Portugal, the military's belief that they could dismiss the elections and their results proved a devastating miscalculation. For the elections subverted their project and marked the beginning of what may be considered a second transition, the logic of which the military finally found difficult to reverse.

In Chile, in a context that could not even be called transitional, Gen. Augusto Pinochet confidently called a referendum on his rule. The referendum produced unexpected effects similar to those of the Portuguese elections; it made it extremely difficult for the dictator to discount his defeat.

In South Korea, in yet another transitional context, unexpected presidential and parliamentary elections untangled a contentious regime crisis that had been developing without clear exits in sight. The elections bestowed a degree of legitimacy on a president who came from the ranks of the old regime, but also compelled him to come to terms with the parliamentary opposition.

Semicompetitive elections in Poland have, in the space of a few weeks, carried political change well beyond anybody's expectations. And even in Central American countries as diverse in regimes as Nicaragua and El Salvador, the mere fact of holding reasonably free elections, though insufficient to steer the countries toward jointly accepted competitive democracies, introduces principles of democratic legitimation that neither the regimes nor, for that matter, their most extreme enemies can easily exorcise.[7]

I take these examples to be a final testimony to the virtue of free elections, and of timing, as tactical signals of firm commitment to the democratic bargain. The next section will essay to show that these signals are also the most desirable among the few available.

TACTICS: WHAT ELSE IS AVAILABLE?

In addition to timing, there is another way in which a firm commitment to the democratic bargain can be made explicit, and that way is through formal pacts. Formal pacts are an extension of the logic whereby informal cooperation in crafting the democratic bargain is beneficial. They have been employed in the older and, more sporadically, in the more recent Latin American transitions, as well in Spain's transition. They are emerging even in Eastern Europe. But there are key questions about what pacts can or should encompass.

Pacts

As to their usefulness, pacts can circumvent in principle (I dare say deny) the prophecy that without habituation democracy is lame. If gradual transitions, which should favor habituation, belong today to a partially mythical past that cannot be recreated, if impatience marks the clock of most transitions, if regime opponents look at gradualism as either meek or self-serving, then it is more advisable to find some "functional" equivalent of habituation that can nullify the prophecy of a lame democracy. Another reason to find equivalents is that, even if the prescription for gradual transitions hides no self-serving agenda, it is still rudderless.

Indeed, if there are no other agendas, then the prescription genuinely wishes to stress the importance of learning, practice, and time, without which tolerance and respect for mutual guarantees cannot get rooted and turned into habits. But the prescription cannot tell us how much time is required or even desirable to develop habits, so therefore it is a sensible but vague prescription at best. More seriously, it suggests at any rate that quite a long time is in order—enough for political institutions and perhaps primary agencies of political socialization to root those habits. More, in other words, than any reasonable time-bound transition can afford. Yet surely transitions are not meant to disseminate pervasive but intangible habits and attitudes, as the prescription implies. They are meant only to make concrete decisions about democratization. Furthermore, as we shall see in the next chapter, the commitment to these decisions may very well be sufficient to adjust subsequent behavior and attitudes accordingly, without the aid of time.[8]

If need be—if democratization takes place in a conflict-ridden context—decisions can be embodied in pacts that will signal a firmer and clearer collective commitment. In this sense, pacts can work as shortcuts to habituation. They can at the very least reduce the interest of any significant actor in "breakdown games"—that is, games designed to prevent or repeal democratization. But in exchange for what? There is no denying that political actors are often extremely reluctant to enter into pacts (which testifies to the importance of their content) and that pacts may have to be drawn with an eye to those who opt to stay out. Reluctance stems from the very real concern with being caught in a lopsided outcome.

Pacts can be lopsided not only by what they do, but also by what they suppress, forbid, and postpone. A pact that results in the latter actions and thus postpones full democratization, is hardly a reassuring early signal. It can hardly be justified by demurrals that it takes time to develop democratic skills, so one needs to go one step at a time. We develop democratic skills only by exercising democracy, not by limiting and postponing it until some purportedly riper times. Chapter 4 deals at length with the virtues of *garantismo* as a set of constitutional rules that facilitate the transfer of loyalties to democracy. The patent implication of *garantismo* is that, if formal pacts are chosen to take the edge off a difficult transition, they should be politically open to participation, so that readiness to cooperate in the elaboration of *garantista* rules is signaled.

To be sure, as politically open as pacts should be, they are employed first of all to introduce restraint, a sense of civility, a curb on violence and aggression (whether by civilians or the state). They are used to provide some orderly exit from divisive times. There exists therefore a whole range of politically motivated behaviors that, though they constitute a resource in the typical arsenals of political and state actors, need to be controlled through pacts—as nearly a prerequisite of democratization. I have in mind behavior motivated by a spectrum of negative sentiments toward democratization—from outright rejection to fear of lopsided outcomes—and employed more to undermine than merely to direct, democratization. It clearly includes state violence and arbitrariness, political persecution, appeals to the military, armed rebellion, and orchestrated strife. Less clearly, it includes mass mobilization, strikes, street demonstrations, and nonviolent disobedience.[9] It makes little sense, for instance, to enter point-blank into an agreement to hold supposedly free elections without a previous understanding, formal or informal, to curb aggressive behavior that would betray the intent of the elections. Similarly, we have already noticed the importance of liberalization before democratization. In this sense, a sequence of pacts may be required, whereby military pacts to stop armed violence and repression precede political ones to undertake democratization.[10]

Nonetheless, it is one thing to constrain politically motivated behavior that clearly undermines democratization. It is another, and much less advisable, to constrain the kind of generically unsettling behavior that accompanies the resurrection of civil society. If at all, constraints in the latter case should be strictly limited to the military pacts where the creation of a peaceful environment for mutual trust is the first and urgent order of business. But past this stage, curbing the ability of parties to operate freely, insisting on complex party licensing procedures, limiting access to political positions and resources, or restraining the parties' capacity for mobilization, and then encasing these controls in elite pacts that favor some actors, leaving others without a voice at crucial founding moments, can produce the unwanted. Those who are left out learn that behavior that disrupts democratization is the most valuable weapon in their political arsenal.

Arguably, no set of political actors—left, right, or center —can be entirely insensitive to the benefits of democratization pacts. But can pacts offer *more*, so as better to allay the reluctance of actors to enter the democratic game? Are pacts for democratization sufficient for all actors? Must they suffice? In addition to procedural guarantees, can and should pacts offer explicit and substantive policy commitments—a material base on which to build acceptance of the democratic game? Though democracy is about uncertainty, there is a minimum of corporate identities, vital to the functional and institutional interests of some transitional actors, not easily subjected to uncertainty. They are not the object of a competitive game; rather, they define the boundaries of the game. Thus, in regard to these identities, procedural guarantees for an unbiased game are not sufficient, and substantive guarantees are invoked to protect corporate spaces. They are guarantees that—to be sure—may channel, indeed limit, a new democracy's future policy choices.

Earlier in the chapter I have signaled as many as three broad constituencies whose accommodation may be central to a successful transition. Though they tend to overlap with, or find representation through, mass political actors (conventionally, the right and left), they can also be identified as functional/institutional actors. They are labor, the state apparatus, and, when transitions occur in a capitalist context, the economic bourgeoisie. Though all three actors are extremely sensitive to substantive policy choices that directly affect their domain, there are reasons why policies accommodating the latter two constituencies may have to take precedence in the transition.

Accommodating Business

Even if the bourgeoisie does not sympathize with the political right to start with, contrary to conventional assumptions,[11] it is fairly intuitive to suggest that its support for democracy rests critically on evidence that the transition intends to protect an economic and public policy environment favorable to business. Without this evidence, the essential fact that the transition may open ample opportunities for democratic representation could still lose much of its appeal. Indeed, in response to its perceived marginalization, those opportunities would become another weapon in the bourgeoisie's arsenal of resistance.

Signs of marginalization and defenselessness are usually

not lacking, especially when transitions escape regime control. Long suppressed labor and economic demands by workers and sectors of the professional middle classes are likely to escalate, if left unchecked, while the regime's shaky economic legacy, international and domestic, leaves the economy in a postdictatorial downturn.[12] A general political climate of resentment or suspicion toward business, and the internal disagreements and external resistance the bourgeoisie may encounter in giving itself a new and effective political identity, may confirm feelings of marginalization.

In addition, entertaining and negotiating the demands of business need not be, and should not be construed as, merely acts of self-defense, unfortunate in their conservative implications, but necessary to secure democracy given the circumstances of most transitions. If, on one side, protecting a market economy may seem, and thus be treated as, a concession to the past, then on the other side such an economy seems a parameter of any operating democracy. No transition from dictatorship has successfully done away with the market without doing away with the prospects for democracy.

Still, what should the accommodation of market and business interests entail? It is fair to assume that political actors will disagree over what should be considered vital to these interests, and that at any rate corporate demands will exceed what is vital in an effort to impose restrictions on labor demands, if not on democratization itself.

Regarding, first, democratization, there is no reason to sacrifice it in the the name of prudent accommodations. Policies can accommodate inherited corporate interests not only by what they specifically contain but also by what they imply and signal: what the policies convey, clearly and in a timely fashion, about the attitude of democracy toward those interests; what they disclose about democracy's commitment to a climate of trust; what they portend about the central role that the interests shall maintain. None of these signals requires placing business (or the state) outside the pale of democratic checks, or assigning either of them a privileged controlling role in the process of democratization beyond the one they can exercise through democratic channels. They largely require facilitating the specific functional and institutional roles of corporate interests; or perhaps they require more simply a hands-off posture toward the interests—one that can make them accept, in return, a counterbalancing (and as such much needed) mobilization of popular strata, focused mainly on the creation of an openly competitive political game.

Signals of an opinion and policy climate favorably disposed toward business are especially important because many transitions inherit a context of domestic and international economic difficulties. Most typical is the Latin American case, where runaway inflation and public and international indebtedness coincide with a crisis of economic development models supplied by regional dictatorships, and where international constraints (for instance, on refinancing debt) mark narrow and costly paths out of the crisis. When the crisis reaches such magnitudes, it is impossible for an emerging democracy to provide a quick fix, even through an illusory exit from the international economic community. Nor can an emerging democracy hope to avert its economic problems by blaming dictatorship, even assuming the blame will stick. Hence, given also that the path out of the economic crisis is narrow, long, uncertain, and invariably arduous, it is meanwhile more important for democrats to build business confidence by focusing on the few signals that are available.

Some of these signals are not actually policies but simply a commitment to avoid certain policies, such as unloading the costs of the economic crisis on business or, worse, holding business politically responsible together with regime leaders for the crisis *and* its political roots. Whether or not the bourgeoisie as a class has had any role in the dictatorship, separate from the role of individuals, a sure way to confirm their reservations about democracy is to cast transition policies, economic or other, as a way to punish them for that alleged role.

Some policies, such as expropriation and nationalization, appear fundamentally punitive, especially in the industrial sector. They are difficult to justify in light of the economic creed that prevails domestically and internationally. Whether or not they have been cast as punitive, the policies are likely to strike a note unquestionably more threatening to corporate identities than, for instance, the banning of nostalgic political parties. By comparison, agrarian and fiscal-financial reforms, if properly presented, can count on at least a degree of economic justification. Moreover, care in the selection of economic measures that are costly to business must be accompanied by signs, not necessarily tangible, that economic recovery is receiving priority attention, that the costs will be shared by other constituencies, and that in any case the new democracy understands the central place of a free economy.

All these considerations suggest, finally, the advantage of *timely* economic pacts not only for sharing sacrifices but also for demonstrating an understanding of the priority of economic recovery. Though military and political pacts for the purpose of reconstituting an environment of civilized political dialogue often demand first attention, an exclusive and prolonged focus on negotiating these pacts, to the detriment of economic ones, may be read variously as a sign of self-centered and myopic powerplays, indecisiveness and ineffectiveness, politicking and unresolved contentiousness—all prejudicial to economic recovery.[13] The latter, for instance, cannot always be left waiting till elections and their manner are agreed upon, votes are counted, alliances are struck, and a prudent assessment is conducted to find out what is politically feasible in dealing with the economic crisis. Instead, prompt attention to economic issues is a frequent way to make functional/institutional interests more accepting of democratic reforms. Further, because economic pacts are negotiated more effectively by cohesive partners, and because organized business may instead find itself in disarray, another useful signal is for democrats to encourage business associationism in a democratic context.[14]

Accommodating the State

Bourgeois reluctance, even disaffection, may not be sufficient to thwart a democratic transition. Yet inattention, real or perceived, to the vital corporate needs of business often coincides with a similar neglect of the corporate needs of the state apparatus, and the armed forces in particular. If democratization may not be stopped by the noncooperation of a broad social group, it may be stopped by a task-oriented state apparatus—one on whose performance society depends and which also masters the means of control and repression. Thus, the corporate concerns of such apparatus, in recycling itself from serving dictatorship to serving democracy, hardly need emphasis.

But paying attention to the concerns of the state need not mortgage democratization, any more than paying attention to business and the market does. The statement applies most clearly to transitions that occur in countries where past constitutional traditions construed the state as the impersonal carrier of specified public functions, indeed duties, in the continuous determination, allocation, and delivery of collective goods. Though the traditions may have been cast originally in an autocratic mold, though they may have assigned civil society and public opinion a narrow legal space, though they may have elevated the state and its armed forces to the role of arbiters of "unnatural" societal conflict, they are still traditions anchored to notions of professionalism, legalism, impartiality, continuity of service, and institutional autonomy from partisan politics—that is, to notions that, whether myth or substance, are central to democracy as well.[15] To some extent, perhaps surreptitiously and willy-nilly, these notions may have lingered on under the dictatorship. Reviving these notions is thus one task of democratic transitions. But there should be no conflict here because the state apparatus may also have a stake in the revival.[16]

It follows that a democratic transition has much to gain if it shows a clear appreciation that armies, judiciaries, civil services—as institutions with legal-rational aspirations—can serve, and are needed to serve, democracy. I have mentioned military pacts as a first step toward reconstituting a peaceful dialogue. They can be extended into institutional pacts, designed to reassert the vital corporate role of those bodies. Assuming that, as likely, the transition is first controlled by the old regime, such reassertion can be decisive in persuading the regime to relinquish control. It can assist a process of secession from the dictatorship. Some state institutions may be tempted to secede in order to regain a legal-professional status stolen from them by a dictatorship that slid into erratic arbitrariness and fitful repression.

As in the case of business, reasserting the state's corporate interests may simply demand staying clear of certain policies: for example, policies that can be construed as retroactive punishment of state personnel *qua* class, rather than as punishment of individuals or necessary removal of specifically repressive legal features added by the dictatorship. There is no denying that, when a regime commits massive abuses, only an imperceptible line may separate individual from collective responsibility. Yet this line must be drawn in the interest of purging the abuses and recovering the state. Other policies may have to be sacrificed to that double interest, such as policies intended to democratize the state apparatus by opening the army, the police, local government, and the judiciary to nonprofessional personnel representing the civilian and armed opposition. Such policies threaten a professional tenet central to the state apparatus: its internal self-rule, its right to enforce and verify, if not to set, criteria for institutional recruitment and advancement. It was a violation of this corporate tenet (the induction into the professional officer corps of nonprofessional *milicianos* because of the colonial wars) that triggered the Portuguese military revolt *against* the dictatorship.

Finally, democratic attention to the corporate needs of the state—and similarly of business—can be helped by one factor. Neither the state nor business is a cohesive whole. Just as state institutions trapped in the descending spiral of a fitfully repressive dictatorship can be divided by the lack of agreement on what to do, so can business lose whatever corporate coherence it possessed when fitful economic experiments (from import substitution to monetarism) fail to deliver the economic recovery on which a dictatorship, or a sequence of dictatorships, based their claim to power.

In both cases, attention to corporate needs can appeal and give leverage to the more daring secessionists; and this in turn can finally have bandwagon effects that help to convert their more cautious colleagues. These effects, the virtues of which we have repeatedly encountered, are another reason why corporate accommodations need not sacrifice political democratization. Corporate interests can better appreciate (better, perhaps, than prudent democrats dare to hope) the advantages of recombining, and ultimately rescuing, themselves in a democratic environment if they can only contrast these advantages with their predicament. The predicament is either to live in the present discomfort of their internal disagreements or to embark in a chancy and costly effort to back out of secession in the vain hope of recovering a lost (or indeed mythical) cohesiveness.[17]

The comments in this section apply well to capitalist states. But what about Communist states? Because of the special problems with reconciling communism's post-totalitarian states (particularly the party apparats that run them) to reforms that would change their identities, the issue deserves, as I've already said, separate treatment later on in this book.

Accommodating Labor

I have argued that, in the interest of democratization, the corporate demands of business and the state may have to take precedence over those of labor, even when labor, after a long period of autocratic repression, may actually be escalating its demands. But what sacrifices are required of labor? What sacrifices can it tolerate without withholding confidence in democracy? Again, labor will be asked to make more sacrifices than are necessary, and labor will concede fewer than it can actually afford. Because declared preferences do not reveal the nonnegotiable bottom line, we need our own assessment of where to strike the bargain.

The assessment is that, from the perspective of labor, economic sacrifices, if called for, are more negotiable than political ones. This is so because there exists a sphere of political action which is central to the identity of labor; indeed, at its core, it is not renounceable. At the same time, from the perspective of a business class called to operate in a capitalist democracy, it is labor's economic restraint that counts more than labor's balancing political gains. Hence the trade-off: labor's economic sacrifices must be compensated—and can be compensated—by democratic political gains.

There exists a significant point of difference between labor and business as collective political actors. Business finds it *convenient* to organize itself as a collective political actor to protect its interest in profit and accumulation. Because profit is necessary for the successful operation of a capitalist system, the political organization of business, though not redundant, is simply expedient. Before becoming a political actor, business is a functional actor. Yet profit, though necessary in order to heed labor's demand for a more equitable share of the wealth it helps to produce, is not at all sufficient to guarantee that share.[18] Therefore, labor finds it *necessary* to organize itself politically. Labor is born a political actor. More simply put, because the material expectations of labor are not satisfied by concessions from the top (least of all in our dictatorships), it follows that labor has a prior paramount interest in its own political organization. It follows also that, for labor more than for business, democracy—as the organization of conflict over material interests—is an obvious and instinctive choice over dictatorship.

I would in fact tentatively extend this statement to labor in Eastern European regimes—where, so to speak, business and the state overlap—as these regimes undergo their own transitions. There is a great concern among political analysts and practitioners that Eastern European labor may not be willing to sacrifice its own "social contract" with those regimes for the sake of democracy and the market.[19] But is the concern overstated? There is no question that reforming Eastern European regimes are calling for unpalatable economic sacrifices. What is not at all clear, however, is whether, as some would have it, resentment at the sacrifices would turn labor into the odd bedfellow of those who defend the command economies of the region and resist wider political changes.

Would labor remain defensively attached to the penurious and leveling security of the social contract? Perhaps, but it is precisely the inability of the command economies to fulfill the promises of the "social contract" that seems at issue in the region; just as the economic model proper of capitalist dictatorships is at issue in the transitions affecting most of the latter. From this may just as well come (one thinks of Solidarity in Poland) the impulse for labor to respond to sacrifices, not by returning to political models within which it has no influence, buy by reasserting, in all transitions, its competitive political autonomy. A different matter is whether and how the apparats that control Communist economies can come to accept the free organization of labor. If in a capitalist economy labor's economic restraint counts more than its political gains, the same does not hold in a collectivized economy.

But labor's vested interest in democracy must be nurtured and rewarded. Though democracy is usually reformist in the long run—having curbed, slowly over its history, business's sway over labor—such may not be the case in the short run. Yet the short run is decisive. We already know that economic reconstruction may require economic sacrifices from labor—the postponement of material demands to an uncertain future. But more generally, uncertainty is the very essence of the democratic game—especially when it comes to labor, whose material demands are made to depend on business profit. This means labor has an added interest—indeed, at its core, a nonrenouceable interest—in seeing that the democratic game is arranged so as to increase the probability of its own influence in the foreseeable future. And the greater the immediate material sacrifices demanded, the greater that interest will be. Plainly, labor has an interest in *garantista* reforms that foster its local and national reorganization, in its union and party components, as a full participant in the democratic game.

Again, because the point of this chapter is how to sell the democratic game before its constitutional design is actually completed, commitment to *garantismo* should be signaled to labor early on. Many features of *garantismo* can be enforced provisionally before they are constitutionalized—just as it is often done, for example, with electoral laws. At the same time, recognition and organizational benefits can be bestowed on labor by transferring to it the resources of government-controlled unions and similar mass organizations operated by the dictatorship. Labor can also be made part of constitutional negotiations, not just on matters of direct labor relevance, but on matters that touch more widely on the distribution of power in society. True, some constitutional reforms favorable to labor may paradoxically not be put to immediate use: for example, the recognition of the right to strike may go together with a request to suspend strike action in the interest of economic reconstruction. But this is not a reason to withhold that recognition, but a reason to extend pacts to the economic sphere—to have labor negotiate its own sacrifices and call its own trade-offs.

From the perspective of business, or the old state apparatus, political reforms may be more than they wished to bargain for. Yet, taken alone, the reforms may not be sufficient to harden their reluctance toward democracy—not unless, in concomitance with or because of some economic faux pas, the reforms signal a special desire to punish and expropriate those corporate interests.

From the perspective of labor, in contrast, political reforms are something more than means to an ultimately material end. They establish the identity of labor as a free political agent. They are its citizenship, indeed its birth right. When they come after years of enforced labor silence, they confer a new sense of collective worth. They also recreate those organizational ties between leaders and followers that, after years of diaspora, labor needs in order to become a cohesive and influential, as well as responsible and legitimate, actor. Therefore, for both labor leaders and followers, the value of newly acquired political rights goes beyond what, in the immediate run, leaders and followers can materially purchase with them. The involvement of labor in democratic affairs, the recovery of its collective voice, can become ends unto themselves, and their material returns do not need immediate verification.

To put it plainly, political democracy can be (and can be made) as attractive for labor, in the short run, as economic equality and social justice.

TACTICS AND THEIR COSTS

Two questions can be raised concerning the trade-off tactics analyzed in the second part of this chapter. The questions reflect legitimate doubts about that analysis. The first one is about the range of cases to which the tactics apply: Are the trade-offs promising and attractive in any or all cases of transition, or are there not limits? The second question is about their possible side-effects: Assuming that the trade-offs obtain a successful transition, are there not lingering costs for the new democracy?

Trade-offs Everywhere?

The answer to the first question is that indeed trade-offs apply to a limited range of cases. Although these limits are not as numerous or as firm as we may think. The suggested trade-offs are part of our ongoing exercise in pushing outward the boundaries of what is possible/plausible. But we have already seen scenarios where the outer boundaries seem to have been reached and where the trade-offs get to be more and more strained.[20] Let us restate these scenarios—with the promise, however, that, being less than totally convinced on the location of the boundaries, we will continue to poke at them until the last chapter.

I have suggested that parasitic state apparatuses should be uninterested in the offer of legal-rational autonomy in exchange for their tolerance of resurrected democratic freedoms: both democratic freedoms *and* legal-rational autonomy are direct threats to the logic of patrimonial appropriation typical of the apparatuses.

Similarly, in a traditional agrarian state, dominated by highly authoritarian and exploitive agrarian relations, landowners are most unlikely to accept the political reorganization of labor. Given the nature of the predominant agrarian relations, labor reorganization would alter much more than the distribution of future profits; it would alter, economically and culturally, those very relations. Further, in states such as these, labor may well reciprocate the lack of interest in trade-offs. The notion of trading immediate material gains against the less tangible advantages of political reorganization loses meaning. For one thing, as just pointed out, labor may well encounter sustained opposition to its political reorganization. For another, in point of fact, there may be little to reorganize, not just because of previous specific repression by the dictatorship, but because traditional economic and social relations work against the associability of labor. Finally, therefore, the political reorganization of labor cannot be pursued in the presence of the traditional corporate interests, but demands a degree of feared transformation of the same.

Leaving aside systemic features of politics and society, trade-offs may also lose attractiveness in extreme transitional scenarios. If something resembling our third, Portuguese scenario were to occur—the old regime is in disarray, comprehensive social reformers are in control of the transition, they inherit in addition a crisis of the dictatorship's economic model that falls on a society scarred by glaring social injustice—we can expect (to restate that scenario) that the temptation will be very strong to jettison as unnecessary the restraints of a democracy with pacts, in fact, of a competitive democracy plain and simple. The temptation will also be to push for radical reforms, and to make the old regime interests pay the bill. At the other extreme, a Brazilian-style transition—slow, without clear signs of underlying crisis, carefully controlled by the old regime in a climate of demobilization that is not conducive to popular pressures—also presents, unfortunately, no clear incentives for trade-offs. Why accommodate labor? Why offer it a special role in the transition? Why indeed change the pace of the transition by calling early elections? Why travel all the way to *garantismo* when the pressures are apparently not there?[21]

Finally, we must remember, that, even aside from the extreme transitional and systemic scenarios just discussed, accommodating corporate interests is not that easy. A case in point is contemporary Latin America, where the total political and moral discredit accompanying the collapse of most military regimes (the exception is Brazil) has left the terms (perhaps even the matter) of the military's accommodation to democracy still open. When the line between the individual and collective responsibilities of the military is difficult to draw, and when there is popular clamor for purges and political reforms, it is difficult for civilian authorities to justify negotiations with the military institutions. It is also difficult for the military to fathom what convenient shape their corporate identity might assume in a democratic context. Similarly, Latin American transitions have been marked by a general failure of business, labor, and government to strike social pacts, especially pacts that would address not only impending economic issues but also the long-range problem of interest organization. While wavering between populist and orthodox policies for dealing with debt and inflation and occasionally making material concessions, now to labor and now to business, the new democratic governments (with the possible exception of Bolivia) have largely failed to bring business and labor together on a broader model of interest intermediation.

Is something objectively inescapable, however, about the latter predicament? In part, the failure to seek agreement may reflect the magnitude and inevitability of the economic crisis, which distract the government from seeking long-range solutions. In part, it may reflect the state of disarray of corporate interests—an understandable one in view of the repression of free interest associationism by the old regimes, and further that during the transition, interest associations may be internally divided, organizationally dispersed, and therefore insensitive to accommodations.[22] In part, however, blame for the predicament is subjectively placed by corporate interests at their governments' doorsteps. For they perceive their governments as unwilling to enter into anything but narrowly reactive, instrumental, and self-serving agreements.[23] And whether or not this diagnosis is fair, given the objective circumstances, it does work as a self-fulfilling prophecy.

But all of this suggests that economic crisis and disorganization of interests should not be seen as insurmountable obstacles to social pacts. On the contrary, crisis and disorganization could just as well convince a government to make the reorganization of corporate interests, and of the structures and rules through which they interact, the object of priority negotiation. If not from Latin America, a good illustration comes actually from a more unexpected quarter. I am referring to the negotiations conducted by the Polish regime and Solidarity in early 1989. The negotiations pursued merely a balance between labor's relative and often implicit restraint on wage-earner and consumer demands and the explicit recognition of labor's institutional role as a union and political movement. Central to the negotiations was, on one side, the desire to move cautiously on both economic and democratic reforms so as to avoid backlashes, but on the other side the recognition that only a politically reconstituted and secure labor movement could carry along its otherwise fragmented followers, reabsorb its intransigent fringes, and thus negotiate sacrifices.

But there is more that is interesting in the Polish case. There is a suggestion that the outer boundaries of what is usually considered as possible/plausible in regard to democratization can be moved further—even beyond where I have been placing them so far. Only months before it started, the Polish dialogue would have been exceedingly hazardous to predict. It would seem logical to argue, for instance, that for a Communist regime, where the party overshadows, or overlaps with, the state, the promise of corporate autonomy for the state holds insufficient appeal to push the regime toward full democratization.[24] And so it may be. Competitive democracy was not exactly what the Polish regime had in mind.[25] I leave for the last chapter the issue of how a reigning (but ruling?) Communist party can be, so to say, negotiated out of its preferences.

Meanwhile, a dialogue is in place, regime and opposition regret the time wasted in years past, and the border between liberalization and democratization is often trespassed. So, if on one side gradualism is emphasized and we may fret that full democracy is not around the corner for Poland, on the other side the desire to negotiate future moves acknowledges, in an unexpected place, the finally discovered importance of pacts and negotiations. Indeed, Spain and its transition through pacts have become a constant point of reference, a code name, in the Polish dialogue, as they are in Hungary and Czechoslovakia. At the same time, emphasis on maintaining the pace of negotiations indirectly acknowledges that gradualism is not without costs. In fact, in the short interval between the time I first wrote these lines and the time I revised them, Solidarity has won elections designed to limit its wins and one of its members has been designated prime minister by a Communist president and confirmed with Communist votes.

Are Trade-offs Too Costly?

Let us return finally to the second question of these conclusions: assuming that prudent trade-off tactics obtain a competitive political democracy for us, are there costs relating to that prudence, and if so, how lingering are they? In fact, given the conservatism that usually accompanies most contemporary transitions to democracy, are the costs typical of all transitions, whether or not they are softened by explicit compromises? The answer is that there are social costs, and perhaps costs in performance—especially in some cases. Whether they are lingering, however, and whether therefore there are also costs in stability, perhaps in legitimacy, is uncertain enough to deserve attention in the next two chapters.

Given the thrust of these pages, there is little doubt that immediate social costs are high when "conservative" transitions—that is, transitions in which reforms are limited to the adoption of the rules for political competition—occur in a society long scarred by social injustice and by a defunct economic model that buttresses that injustice. The social costs become greater when these political transitions, as a reflection of their social conservatism, also call for pacts that impose further social restraint and economic sacrifices on the popular sector. And the costs are even greater when the material sacrifices required by the pacts are not compensated by official support for the political reorganization of the popular sector.

The implication would seem to be that conservative transitions should produce conservative democracies: their future performance presumably being confined by the starting conditions. And this should have negative consequences for the life of those democracies. There are indeed a number of good reasons why this may be so; but there are also good reasons why it does not have to.

On the side of pessimism, we can expect that resistance to significant alterations in society's authoritarian relations would continue under a conservative democracy, both because those relations are regarded by some dominant groups as vital to their life-styles and because the expectation that those relations will be preserved is part of those groups' acceptance of political democracy.[26] We can expect, in turn, that democratic governments confronted with such expectations would, out of fear, move very cautiously on social reforms, and would in fact invite backsliding. We can expect a corresponding disenchantment with democracy in the popular sector. We can expect a poor environment for democratic growth, for democracy fares better if society provides greater areas for civic participation and communal interaction. We can expect, finally, that these strands will converge to place democracy, stilted and precarious in its performance, at serious risk. The chain of argument is familiar; it is a variation on the theme that democracy does not grow in the soil of social inequalities, even if we manage to plant it there.

But does it have to be so? Let me broaden the question. Let me move from conservative transitions to any transition that, for any reason, has experienced difficulties. In some cases the difficulties may be linked to inauspicious social conditions, in other cases to the very circumstances of the transition. In some transitions the difficulties may reside in their conservatism; in others, dominated by comprehensive social reformers, they may reside in excessively ambitious radicalism; in yet other transitions, neither clearly conservative nor radical, the difficulties may reside in the generic problem of finding a mutually agreeable balance in constitutional or social choices. Whatever the case may be, the broader question is whether transitions that experience difficulties mortgage future performance so heavily that democracy is caught in a vicious circle. Is there a vicious circle, or can the difficulties be dealt with, in the life of a democracy?

The essay's emphasis on *garantismo* and this chapter's emphasis on pacts strong on mass/political overtures are meant to stress that the democratic game is not foreclosed, that it can be played to greater advantage as democratic life unfolds, and that at any rate it is the only reformist game; the only one able to protect the waging of social conflict for the purpose of altering social relations. If democracy does not guarantee that the relations shall be altered, it does not guarantee their preservation either.

If we can argue convincingly that a democracy is not entirely doomed by a difficult birth, there is then more than a gleam of hope for its future performance. The argument is part of the next chapter.

CHAPTER VI

Beyond Transitions
Why Democracy Can Deliver on Its Promises

Crafting democratic rules—crafting them collectively and expeditiously—is not an easy task. But once the rules have been attended to, democratic life assumes a significantly different, sturdier, quality.

The thesis of this chapter is simple. When an agreement on democratic rules is successfully reached, the transition is essentially over. Democracy enters a new phase in which the behavior of the actors is influenced, to an extent not seen before, by the presence of the new rules. The effect is double: (1) The new rules constitute a compelling, more civilized guide for the expression and handling of communal conflict. They cannot be easily overlooked. (2) The rules are not so rigid, however, as to prevent their adjustment over time. Nor are they intended to fully dictate the performance of democracy and the outcomes of communal conflict. Indeed, by agreeing to the rules, political actors agree that performance and outcomes will be uncertain to some degree.

Each of the two effects has a potentially positive function. On the one hand, the adoption of a civilized discourse signifies that greater confidence is built in the stability and viability of mutual security. On the other, the pliability of democratic rules and their somewhat open effects leave room for improvement within mutual security; this is also a way to build confidence in the democratic game.

There is a familiar counterargument to my claim; to wit, just as it takes time to craft an agreement, so it takes time and habituation before the agreement is secure and any danger of failure, stemming from the transition or its antecedents, is removed. Thus, unless we were to define rule agreement in a way that suits the claim, the decision to agree on a set of rules is not sufficient to reorient collective behavior significantly and does not constitute a turning point.

This counterargument reasons from a sensible kernel: habituation, accompanied as it is by the testing and rooting of institutions, must play a role—although a difficult one to assess—in building viability and confidence. Still, it is the initial agreement on rules that is decisive for removing the danger of failure. When political actors agree on a set of democratic rules, we can take this as a sign that, for whatever reason (conversion, but more simply, and more likely, a fall in disruptive resources), those among them who were bent on "breakdown games" have now lost interest in them, or have become marginal, less capable of rallying support from sympathizers, or less likely to trigger similarly destabilizing defensive responses from adversaries equally contemptuous of democracy. Further and more to the point, the more expeditious the agreement, the better it is. Only when the agreement is reached can the new and more promising phase—buttressed by the agreement—begin in earnest. This is generally labeled a phase of consolidation. But if we follow the prevailing term, we should not attach a surfeit of meaning to the word; the decisive role in establishing democracy belongs to the agreement phase, not to consolidation.

It should be clear that an agreement that halts breakdown games and opens a new phase of testing and adjustment may have to be something more than the agreement of a simple majority. If the object is to make sure that no significant actors are left out—that is, no actors who, by staying out, can continue to endanger the agreement—then any agreement, even if it does not formally include those actors, must at the very least be drawn with an eye to co-opting them. Or, in fact, a broader, more composite, more patently collective agreement may at times be needed.[1] Not surprisingly, this is the type of agreement whose emergence is favored by the transitional choices and tactics of *garantismo* and pact making. If the agreement does not include, or is not drawn with an eye to, significant actors, then single democratic institutions may well be adopted and put to work. But their effectiveness and persuasiveness—their capacity eventually to co-opt those who stayed out of the agreement —are in jeopardy.

Still, nothing more is expected of the agreement beyond the requirement that no significant actors be overlooked. Because the reasons and motives leading to the agreement are as diverse as the political actors, the agreement does not always entail the achievement of normative legitimacy. The object of negotiating democratic rules with reluctant actors is not to convert them point-blank but to affect their behavior.

True, we should be mindful of Hirschman's warning about the drawbacks of paths to development that rely on behavioral changes that precede attitudinal ones. Although such paths are more common and successful than we think, when political actors trespass, intentionally or not, into new behavior (for instance, holding free or nearly free elections) before consonant attitudes develop, the path to development "will be more halting and circuitous," tensions between old and new attitudes may well persist, and the "development profile and experience cannot but bear the marks" of the path that was followed.[2] From our perspective, however, the important point, and Hirschman's contribution, is that development can still proceed without waiting for attitudinal change; the latter is not a requisite. Indeed, attitudinal change to remove dissonance between old attitudes and new behavior may not always occur. Meanwhile, the first and contingent choice of trespassing can induce the trespassers to yet other behavioral commitments, with further unanticipated consequences of their own. In this way, actors come to comply with the results of actions that they had taken earlier in the process with other intents and expectations.[3]

LIVING BY THE AGREEMENT

Political actors who subscribe to democratic rules may differ in their motives but have one thing in common: they have subscribed to the rules. This has implications for the chances of reviving breakdown games and for the quality of conflict in the new phase. Once the new democratic rules have been recognized—once the prospects of emerging from the transition with some more hybrid regime, most agreeable to some political actors but least to others, have been set aside (albeit for calculus)—those prospects, and with them the prospects of reviving breakdown games, should get dimmer and roundabout. The drama of impending failure should recede. This new phase is new because it imposes previously less significant constraints on the revival of breakdown games and new incentives to focus on the more constructive democratic game.

The first constraint is the very collectiveness of the agreement to adopt new rules—the decision whether to enter into or exit from the agreement is influenced by what other actors do about it. Just as reluctant actors may have reasons for being included in the agreement when support for it increases, so they also may have reasons (despite their inclination to reconsider) for not being the first ones to abandon it. A move to scuttle the agreement might eventually rescind it, or may isolate the perpetrators. It may leave them out of what is emerging as the only game in town. The more, therefore, the game goes on, and the more actors practice it, the more costly it seems not to play it. If nothing else, there may be no other or safer way of attending to one's interests. So, if Dahl's costs of tolerance and cooperation are of concern to some political actors before they consider the agreement, afterward it is the cost of intolerance and repression that should worry them more.

The behavior of Communist parties in postwar Western Europe aptly illustrates this process of behavioral adaptation to first choices, an adaptation to which the parties have at times consciously contributed. Undeniably, because it has nonetheless taken some time for the Communist parties to practice the game fully and without afterthoughts, the path of democratic development has shown idiosyncrasies. But a mix of subjective reasons, motives, and calculations can be found in various degrees behind practically every existing democracy. Further, the mix of reasons is not only a mix of different actors but also a mix inside single actors.

Closely connected with the constraint just discussed, the new phase also offers inducements to move away from breakdown games. The more costly it becomes to exit from the agreement, the more the partners to the agreement, even reluctant ones, will be motivated to focus their attention on the actual operation of emerging rules and institutions.

Whatever reservations they may nurture, they will formulate them in the spirit of those rules and in view of what they promise. Thus the agreement will be progressively tested, with still some drama but with fewer actual risks, on democracy's own terms and within the democratic compromise. In this sense, too, a decision to revert to breakdown games requires justification of a special sort. In other words, measuring the agreement against institutional performance is a cause of uncertainty (of voice), but not one of necessary instability (of exit).[4]

Another inducement to move away from breakdown games is that, in the new phase, the political actors and the political agenda change in ways that strengthen the relevance of democratic processes for both. In the first place, the political arena, which at first tends to be occupied by elites and selectively mobilized constituencies exploiting positional, legal, professional, charismatic, or military advantage, is now shared with social and political formations sensitive to electoral and mass appeals. In the second place, the political arena is now regulated by a set of democratic rules, therefore democratic state institutions also join in as a significant part, indeed the gatekeepers, of the arena. In the third place, the emergency tasks of the transition proper (the reestablishment of law and order, the removal of the dictatorship and its institutional residues, the search for a democratic agreement, the accommodation of vital corporate interests) are progressively overshadowed by activities concerned with group positioning, institutional routinization, and in sum the definition of how the democratic game is actually unfolding, how rules are working out, and how benefits are distributed. Thus, finally, the originally overloaded and cramped agenda gives way to a decisional process that is better timed, more normal, more informed, and more attentive to recognizable and socially sanctioned groups and institutions.

It is in good part because of these developments that the political actors' time perspectives on performance tend to become more relaxed, as we shall soon see, than they were during the transition. In the midst of the transition, when an agreement is still being sought, time seems to be of the essence, if not for all actors then at least for those who seek a democratic exit. Afterward, the justified desire to cut time short, or at least to set precise deadlines, tends to be replaced by an equally justified appreciation that, to prove itself, the agreement deserves and can afford more measured tempos in keeping with the typical give-and-take of the newly begun democratic process.

But the final and most important inducement to shift actors' attention toward the democratic game resides in what is special about its rules. Democratic rules are special in two ways. In the first place, political actors know that the rules do not concern themselves directly with outcomes, that agreeing on the rules is agreeing mostly on procedures and institutions, that each procedure and institution will impinge on outcomes only partially and probabilistically; in sum, political actors know that performance is not meant to mirror the agreement faithfully. That is why the process of entering into the agreement is surrounded by obstinate jockeying and wrangling. But that is also why, once the agreement is reached, the discovery that outcomes may occasionally vary from what the agreed-upon rules may have led one to expect should not engender necessary dismay and rejection. The agreement could still endure and thus continue to gather support.

In turn, democratic rules justify and reward patience. And this is the second way in which such rules are special. Plainly, they open the political arena to participation and the airing of political demands, they process demands through various institutions (rather than make them fall on one dictator, one

junta, one party), they let public opinion register disagreement by voting out the government rather than overthrow-
ing the regime. If these political practices contribute to a
climate of apparent political instability and democratic irre-
soluteness, they also function as safety valves defusing resentment and dispersing its targets. In fact, they do more.
By distributing decisions among various institutions, the new
practices call for a mixture of repetitive conflict-and-coop-
eration games.

The mixture, the availability of multiple decisional channels, and the opportunity to adjust and repeat decisions all
improve the chances of producing decisional equity—or,
perhaps more important, they increase the perception that
such chances exist. Closely in keeping with the perception is
the propensity to base the assessment of democratic performance on something broader and more elastic than the satisfaction of individual demands.[5] Because democratic decisions emerge out of aggregation, elimination, reformulation,
deferment, give-and-take, the mixture of conflict and cooperation that often surrounds these processes is not only about
which demands should be entertained and which deferred
but also about how the processes should be conducted, what
role the contestants located in and out of government should
play, what symbolic or tangible side-rewards the losers should
reap. It is the conduct of processes, as much as their outcomes, that actors will focus on in order to evaluate performance. Thus their evaluation will be broad and encompassing, both with respect to the evidence it relies on and the
time span it covers. Once again, with this span the democratic agreement can continue to gather support.

There are unmistakable problems of habituation to the
new tempos of democracy, as there are problems with its
give-and-take. Scholars are often impressed by dramatic cases
of democratic collapse, such as Spain's second republic, Ita-

ly's pre-Fascist democracy (1919–21), or the Weimar Republic, and cite them as evidence that many political actors remain unwilling to adopt a long-range perspective on democracy's achievements, that their impatience can converge even as they may oppose each other, and that therefore democracy, with its moderate-to-reformist perspectives, can prove itself inadequate. But, before drawing such conclusions, we should take equal note of those cases where reformist perspectives prevailed.[6] These cases are often rather uneventful, and their diminished newsworthiness does not invite attention. In the folds of nonevents (or of deceptive events), we may yet discover that the new tempos demanded by democracy are well understood by those who have already entered into the agreement.

In fact, sensitivity to the investment made by entering into the agreement and reluctance to scuttle the democratic experiment prematurely are not always uneventful achievements. At times their presence is brought to light by salient episodes that, at first, suggest quite a different turn of events. I have in mind episodes, such as an attempted coup, that threaten the agreement, but by so doing may actually rally around the agreement the other political forces. The usual expectation, well illustrated by the denouement of the second Spanish republic, is that such episodes of destabilization set in dramatic motion a spiral of escalating events. If, let us say, the military threatens a coup, then the popular sector will respond in kind and democratic moderates will waffle and backslide, triggering a polarization that reveals how weakly most actors are committed to the democratic game and how ineffective the game can be. Against this plausible scenario there stands, however, the fact that not all episodes of destabilization come out this way. But, again, these are precisely the episodes that are more easily forgotten because the drama is unfulfilled.

We should also not forget that, if a coup or any other destabilizing event has greater chances of succeeding before an agreement on the rules is reached, these chances should diminish afterward. In this sense, another episode from Spain's history, the attempted coup of 1981, proved in some fundamental ways ill-timed, in that, though it came at a moment of serious internal crisis of the centrist governing party, it also came well after a broad constitutional agreement had been reached. Thus the coup had the effect of strengthening democratic resolve in the government and all other significant actors. It can be argued that the coup lacked credibility and full military support to start with. But this is part of the point I wish to make. The emergence of an agreement on democratic rules (to which the military or some of its sectors may in fact have directly or indirectly contributed) should discourage, as a starter, new breakdown games, given their diminishing chances of support.

Indeed, the record of military coups against reconstituted democratic governments illustrates well why the governments are more resilient than generally expected. Many coups are threatened, not all threats are serious, and only some of the serious ones succeed. The reason is the military's traditional reluctance to engage in coup activities unless prodded by significant civilian constituencies in a context of spreading social and political disintegration. Without such prodding, military conspiracies can prove insubstantial and ineffective.[7] Such may be the case if conspiracies resurface after a properly constituted democratic government is in place; then, the conspiracies not only may rekindle democratic support even among reluctant popular sectors but may also find little response among the military itself and its old civilian allies.

In sum, the investment placed in democracy by entering into the agreement may, to be sure, invite disenchantment later on, as has happened even in the most successful of recent democratizations. Also, little will go without turmoil in the processes I have been describing. Because the agreement is in many ways a means to an end, and for many actors a second-best option, political actors will try to bend it in their favor, using performance as a basis for their claims. It is therefore naive to expect that political actors who managed to reach rule agreement through much struggle will suddenly convert to peaceful, orderly, and uneventful politics. Rather, the task of maintaining the agreement will still be accompanied by its own share of confrontation, tension, and animosity—a target of which is performance. Yet a charged political atmosphere, just like signs of disenchantment, should not be confused with an impending crisis of the agreement, or with what we may classically call a crisis of both performance and legitimacy. Such an atmosphere is indeed common to practically all new democracies and should be kept separate from accomplishments. The expectations vested in the agreement may produce later disenchantment, but they also counsel prudence before scuttling the agreement as defective.

Peter McDonough, Samuel Barnes, and Antonio López Pina have reported recently that Spaniards who show sympathy for the Franco regime are not necessarily averse to the new democracy. Spaniards in general look at the two regimes as distinct experiences, the more so as time goes by, and judge them on the basis of different clusters of orientations toward government.[8] The opinion data were collected following the conclusion of the Spanish constitutional process and during a period that covered an attempted coup as well as the advent of a new Socialist government. The fact that, at least in Spain, attitudes toward the past did not hold the key to the present fits well with the thrust of our argument.

Political actors may respond to democracy, or to specific

democratic institutions and accomplishments, on their own terms—or indeed in view of the times within which a new democracy happens to fall: times of prosperity, of international support for democracy, or of lowering expectations (or their opposite). Nor does adjustment to democracy demand extended attitudinal change so that feelings toward the old dictatorship be made more consonant with feelings toward the new democracy. Even as feelings remain dissonant, I wish to suggest that—if democracy or the times have indeed made the past, past—lingering nostalgia, while cushioning those who have deserted the past, may prove to be a less than forceful guide to present behavior.

There is a note of caution in the conditional form of the last statement. Making sure that the past is past, irrelevant, and obsolete—and, similarly, making sure that the temptation to try new forms of dictatorship or guided democracy remains inoperative—is in good part the task of democratic government. Nothing I have said so far invites democratic governments to be complacent. Despite the great importance assigned to the presence of a democratic agreement, nothing ensures that democratic governments will avoid excessive complacence, boldness, or fear. It is still possible that, by their mistakes, governments will set in motion a breakdown spiral that other political actors will exploit. The cumulation of unresolved issues, especially if a new democracy has a limited capacity to address them forcefully or without sacrifices, must be a matter of constant monitoring by democratic governments.

This is not just because democratic leaders would know the real extent of the threat only after the facts but especially because (whether or not the threat exists, whether or not public opinion has a case against government) good governance, as finally judged by public opinion, is what democratic government is all about. For all the leeway tolerated in performance, for all the starting credit democratic government may enjoy, for all the benefits it may draw from international support or the temper of the times, for all the psychological investment involved in the original agreement, democratic consent is also a reflection of performance, and democracies seek to renew that consent.

This section has listed some of the reasons why, as democracy moves beyond transition, political actors may be led to stay in the game and renew their consent. With performance in mind, I now wish to pursue one of the reasons in greater detail.

IMPROVING THE AGREEMENT

Under democracy, the game is not foreclosed. Democratic rules, I have suggested, are pliable in two ways. Their effects are somewhat open, and the rules can themselves be subject to adjustment over time. The effects of rules are open for many, already known, reasons. To wit, rules, being about competition, do not decide directly and entirely who will exercise decisional leverage but set the standards for measuring and legalizing that leverage. The simplest example is electoral rules, which declare the criteria for victory and in so doing may make it more or less difficult for some group (or some ways of associating) to win elections, but do not handpick the winners. In addition, the rules tend to disperse decisions among multiple decisional channels. As a result of these two qualities, the rules are also open—that is, not entirely determining—with regard both to specific policy outcomes and to who stands to win or lose from the outcomes. Finally, not only are the effects of rules open but also the rules themselves are not meant to be rigid, and circumstances may not allow them to be. Rules may tolerate, more in some cases than in others, a whole range of adaptations—from fine tuning and reinterpretation to renegotiations.

By being pliable in these various ways, democratic rules make it possible to improve both democratic performance and support. The possibility of improvement is another measure of the degree to which entering into an agreement is a turning point in democratic normalization. In contrast, (to state the obvious in order to make a point with which I shall conclude this chapter), there can be no room for improvement unless an agreement already exists.

Let us keep in mind that the agreement we are discussing is one that removes breakdown games; that, for this purpose, the agreement may have to be drawn with an eye to co-opting political actors who have an interest in those games; and that, in turn, co-optation is favored by drawing on *garantismo* and by pursuing expeditious pacts. For I am suggesting that agreement so fashioned is more likely to prove itself pliable in the ways I just described. Once again, the analysis takes a normative turn.

Rules Have Open Effects

A known problem with convincing reluctant or uncertain political actors to accept democratic rules is, not so much the rules themselves, but that the rules' ability to deliver a fair balance of wins and losses can be proved only in the future—past the transition. I have spoken in this sense of a borrowed, or presumptive, legitimacy. But, as we move past the transition, the future is, so to speak, with us. Democratic rules can finally give account of themselves and their promises. This is the time to prove that the decision to enter into the democratic agreement, a decision that carries an initial psychological investment and from which it is difficult to backtrack, can also pay off—despite, at times, some starting conditions that threaten the agreement's ability to deliver.

Let us then take, as a demanding mental test, instances of difficult transitions. Let us see some of the ways in which the openness of the democratic game can still be rescued and can overcome, early on in the course of democratic life, some of the confining conditions. All we need to do is to retrace a line of argument to which I had promised to return.

One frequently expressed concern with recent transitions is the conservative context within which, given the guarded attitudes of political actors in general and the weight of nostalgic forces among political actors, most transitions take place. The concern, as described, extends to the use of pacts as transitional devices. For, while pacts ease the transition, they also seem to give public chrism to halting further democratization in politics, economics, and society. Although the concern has ample grounds, not all the ground is hallowed. For one thing, the concern belittles the function of some pacts in rescuing openness.

In the first place, the absence of pacts is not always a good sign. True, it may reflect a less reluctant and constrained transition, for which pacts are not needed. But, for all the alleged conservatism of pacts, absence may also reflect a state of affairs with even stronger conservative implications. For example, the old regime may still rely on its ability to guide a slow and guarded transition, society may be fraught with inequalities and ingrained authoritarian values, or the popular sector may be disorganized and demobilized. Any or all of these conditions, by convincing the old regime that pacts are largely unnecessary, may foreclose further democratization much more than pacts would. After all, pacts imply the presence of opponents who cannot easily discount each other, the need to accommodate this state of affairs, some disposition to recognize the need,[9] and some ability to respond to it.[10]

In the second place, there are conservative pacts, and then

there are conservative pacts. Some of them are intended not only to fall short of immediate democratization but also in fact to relegate democratization to some unknown future at best. I have argued that such pacts, rationalized by the need for habituation to democratic practices or some similar claim, hold little promise. But the pacts to which my preference and attention have gone—pacts in which immediate socio-economic sacrifices and the postponement of reforms in society, the economy, and the state are nevertheless compensated by official support, even assistance, in the reorganization of the popular sector—hold much greater promise. Intentions notwithstanding, they cannot, by themselves, freeze the future. Strictly speaking, their emphasis on the political reconstruction of the popular sector removes, instead, any assurance that democratic performance will continue to be constrained, let alone determined, by the conservative expectations of weighty constituencies in society or the state.

This claim is nothing but a special extension of the fact that in democracy no set of interests can be secured, and entering into a democratic agreement (the more so if it is one with strong *garantista* components) means accepting the need to compete for, and to share, decisional leverage with other collective interests. Thus, making the agreement part of a pact that also calls for conservative sacrifices and postponements is still no fail-safe way of securing conservative interests beyond a vital core. These are good reasons why the popular sector can place confidence in the democratic agreement, including one that calls for immediate material sacrifices.

It goes without saying that uncertainty is for everyone. There is no guarantee that democratic performance will be confined by the conservative bias, but there is no guarantee that it will go beyond the bias either. Even so, I am afraid there is a tendency to overplay the evidence that original biases persist. Suppose that conservative policies were to continue. Shall we take this as prima facie evidence that a new democracy is the prisoner of an original bias? We should not.

Consider the very real possibility that, as democratic life unfolds, the popular sector—now with its own electoral and organizational leverage—or some parts of the sector come to accept, and indeed to negotiate, the continuation of a program of economic austerity and labor restraint. Is it because putting a stop to the program would risk the resumption of breakdown games, or because of political weaknesses of the popular sector vis-à-vis its adversary, or because the popular sector has come to look at the program as plain "good policy"?

Or consider the possibility that politico-institutional reforms designed to make democracy more democratic (good examples are regional autonomies, lifting government monopoly of the airwaves, instituting police review boards) make no progress. Is it because the reforms find resistance among nostalgic constituencies, or because the democratic forces, for electoral or other reasons of their own, are divided over them?

Consider also the possibility that, under such circumstances, political parties traditionally linked to the popular sector win the elections and replace the government under which the original democratic agreement was reached. Chances are that some of the bickering will now occur between democratic forces, and even within the governing forces and their social constituencies; chances also are that some constituencies will stand accused of caving in to conservative pressures. What shall we make of the bickering and the accusation? And what shall we make of the electoral victory?

In one exemplary case to start with, that of post-Franco

Spain, these or similar developments do not suggest a frozen democratic performance or an ensuing waning of democratic support. In some ways, they suggest the opposite.[11] The Spanish transition was conservative in many of the meanings we have employed here. But, judging by the spectrum of the forces to which it paid attention, it was also open and consensual. The *Pactos de la Moncloa* and the constitution-making process combined these elements quite clearly. Economic sacrifices, labor restraint, and politico-institutional and economic reforms limited by the desire to preserve vital private and state corporate interests[12] went hand in hand with a negotiated constitution strong on *garantismo*, and with an approved reconstruction of the left in its party and labor components. The presence of the latter guarantees meant in turn that the presence of conservative sacrifices, the effort to co-opt the left in the process of democratization (sacrifices included), and the success of the first elected Spanish government in pursuing these strategies all proved insufficient to contain the growth of the left.[13] Less than seven years after the death of Franco, the Socialist party was in power, where it remains.

Of all the signs that a new democracy is consolidating its support, perhaps the strongest and also one of the most difficult to come by[14] is a peaceful government turnover. By this criterion, Spain has done well, and according to some analysts surprisingly well. So has the left. It could be argued that the success of the left, if success it is, carried a cost in democratic performance: to make their victory acceptable, the Socialists had to adopt the conservative bias. But the adduced evidence is improper, and the argument specious. True, the policies of the Socialist government, compared with those of the previous government, are remarkable not for their innovation but for their incrementalism. True, the realities of the international and domestic economies of the last decade have defined the terrain on which the left can move, in Spain as elsewhere. True, radical reformism has lost its historical cachet.[15] But does it all mean that if the Socialist government were to act otherwise, breakdown games would resume? More precisely, does it mean that fear of such resumption is what guides Socialist policies and that, without the fear, government choices would be different? Does it mean that the sacrifices extracted from the left during the transition are still operative and unshakable? None of the evidence warrants such conclusions.

Pacts and negotiations of the type involved in the Spanish transition extract sacrifices for a precise purpose that is tied to the transition. They serve to reach mutual security more successfully. It is a measure of their success that they speed up the resumption of a normally competitive game—including government turnover—and that, with its resumption, some of those sacrifices lose their original constitutional purpose. Of course, part of the game (and part of what makes the principle of alternation in government acceptable) is that governments adhere to certain norms of restraints before deciding to undo each other's work. Behaving otherwise would betray the expectations that are built in the democratic bargain. Thus democratic restraint should not be taken as succumbing to continuing blackmail. Succumbing implies that democracy and its performance continue to be at issue. It is possible that certain historical junctures will push governments (any government) toward a conservative version of the democratic bargain and that efforts to change it will produce meager policy results. But are democracy and its performance thereby at issue?

The Spanish case advises prudence when choosing evidence that should support such notions. Indeed, Spain is a

good example, if not an easy one to replicate, of how confining conditions linked to the transition can be lifted, and
how entering into the democratic agreement can pay off.

I have stressed that the occurrence of a peaceful change
of government, the consolidation of democratic support, and
the freeing of democratic performance from confining conditions were all facilitated, in Spain, by reliance on *garantismo* and pact making. But even without such reliance, and
always provided that a democratic choice has been made,
similar developments are not necessarily foreclosed by an
otherwise difficult transition.[16] To take another southern
European example from the mid-1970s, such a democratic
choice was firmly present in the Greek transition to democracy.

The Greek case is an interesting combination of promises
and emerging difficulties. On one side, the achievement of
full-fledged political democracy, following the military's de-
volution of power to a civilian government headed by Kon-
stantinos Karamanlis, met with little effective recalcitrance,
either from the military (although a number of leaders of
the old junta received hefty prison sentences), or from other
nostalgics (although the monarchy was repealed in a national referendum), or from the left. Despite rumblings and
an attempted coup by sectors of the military, the choice of
democracy was expeditious and in some ways less contro-
versial or belabored than elsewhere in southern Europe. On
the other side (most likely, in retrospect, precisely because
the lesser original recalcitrance made such measures less important) something was missing; there was no pact making,
no consensual constitution making, and no special emphasis
on *garantismo*. The constitution was drafted and adopted
unilaterally by a conservative majority over the resistance of
the left to its neo-Gaullist semipresidential features and to
an electoral law assigning bonus seats to larger parties. Such

constitutional features exhibited qualities of confining conditions. They seemed designed to extend the rule of Karamanlis and his party, also by eroding traditional parties of the political center, and to quarantine the strongest party of the left, the Panhellenic Socialist movement (PASOK). But as in Spain, the Socialists found themselves in power only seven years after the fall of the dictatorship.

It seemed at the time of constitution making that Karamanlis, by cutting the left from the constitutional process and trying to reduce through the electoral law the chances of the left to govern, made a Socialist victory not only less likely but also more traumatic.[17] But the latter forecast proved to be as incorrect as the former. It overlooked the fact that the Socialist movement's acceptance of democracy, by the time of its victory, counted for more than its dissatisfaction with the strong majoritarian slant given to Greek democracy.[18] In fact, the advent of the Socialist government generated a climate of greater confidence in the new democracy. Because the Socialists won by the existing rules, the change in government showed that the confining conditions introduced by the constitutional choices of the transitional government were not insurmountable; it showed further that the rules could be adapted to the new governing context; and thus it showed that the right could coexist with a governing left.

But the reference to the adaptability of democratic rules makes the Greek case interesting in another way. Greece will be one illustration that democratic rules are pliable for yet another reason: not only because their effects are open but also because they can be reinterpreted and redefined.

Rules Are Adaptable

No matter how detailed the terms of the democratic agreement are—and often they should not or need not be—it will look one way on paper and another way once implemented. Translating the terms of the democratic settlement into institutional roles and routines is a prolonged process, and its outcome is somewhat open. Eventually we may arrive at a point when the operation of democratic institutions and processes becomes routinized and predictable, as well as weightier, and therefore more difficult to change. But that point comes well after the democratic agreement is first reached. Meanwhile, because institutions and processes are not yet fixed, it is possible even to change and improve—at times explicitly, at times implicitly or surreptitiously—some of the agreement's original terms.

That rules can be adapted and even changed is fairly clear when the agreement involves mainly political actors with a democratic bias.[19] But the possibility also exists, more importantly, when the agreement co-opts reluctant actors. In the latter case, reluctance may surround the agreement and its terms with substantial fuzziness. Actors may haggle over those terms and their implementation in processes and institutions, thus revealing the constrictions of the agreement as well as the contrasting expectations and divergent interpretations it engenders. But such difficulties do not imply that a modus vivendi is ruled out. The fact that an agreement exists, fuzzy though it is, and the commitment to mutual adjustments that this implies, help a modus vivendi. As illustrated by democratizations in southern Europe, a number of possibilities are conceivable, from perfecting the agreement to making a virtue out of its imperfection.

One possibility is that some important part of the original constitutional settlement is explicitly amended before it takes full hold. Supervening developments—a significant electoral victory, the rise of a new party, and similar events that alter the balance of power and influence—may offer the opportunity. One example is Greece, as it went from a conservative to a Socialist government following the Socialists' decisive electoral victory. What appeared to be a democratic system slanted in a presidential direction that was unappealing to the Socialists of PASOK has evolved into a fully accepted, more genuinely parliamentary system, allowing also for a more proportional electoral law. True, this required institutional reforms at the sufferance of the conservatives; nevertheless, neither the reform nor its aftermath has the makings of a serious constitutional conflict. Both conservatives and socialists have converged on a middle ground.

Another possibility is that, at a minimum, contrasting expectations and interpretations and uncertainties about the concrete shape of the agreement, will disappear in due time more or less of their own accord. This will happen not with explicit decisions or dogged renegotiations, but probably by a process of informal accommodations. As the democratic agreement is implemented, routinization socializes political actors, clarifies norms, and reshapes roles beyond original prospects. Again, and in addition, supervening political developments may contribute to such clarification.

Spain is a good example. Once the transition was over, especially after the Socialists' victory, Spain has settled into a sort of majoritarian government that is quite removed from the *garantismo* and the pact making of the transition, with their emphasis on consensus and cooperation.[20] The constitutional features that, in keeping with the spirit of the transition, adumbrated *garantismo*, have been reconciled with, and toned down by, majority rule. But this evolution was not clear at the time of the transition. Would *garantismo* and broad interparty cooperation become a durable feature of Spanish democracy, as they became in Italy? Would they be the instrument by which the governing UCD (Union of the Democratic Center) would extend its soft hegemony over Spanish politics? Would they become dated, or should they maintain relevance? Different political forces had different expectations. Retrospectively, the outcome proved that the *política de consenso* had succeeded and, by succeeding, had made its painstaking pursuit no longer necessary. And the passage to a majoritarian style of government demanded not constitutional rethinking, but an adaptation of the democratic agreement to the improved circumstances.

A third possibility, exemplified by Italy, is to improve on an imperfect and uncertain agreement by learning to live with its defects, preserving uncertainty in fact and using it for coexistence. In postwar Italy the terms of the constitutional agreement were actually couched broadly so as to increase their attractiveness and the collective interest in entering the democratic game. Heavy on *garantismo*, but otherwise sketchy and noncommittal on the touchier matter of governance, the agreement could still have evolved as it did in Spain: in a majoritarian direction. But although it alleviated the effects produced by reluctance of the extremes, *garantismo* could not fully remove, contrary to Spain, reluctance itself. Thus, when the Communist party emerged as the second political force in the country, the response to the apparent stalemate (an intriguing response in its beneficial effects on coexistence) has been to accept the uncertainty and fuzziness of the original agreement, to agree to disagree on its terms, and to continue to argue—in particular on the roles of government and opposition. The result is a continuous stretching of the agreement that, while ostensibly unsettling, leaves nobody out.

Trying to clarify and pin down the terms of a democratic agreement once and for all, or trying to alter them, may have costs that are not always palatable or necessary. Somebody could be required to make sacrifices that were previously buried in the agreement. In addition, as happened with the sudden emergence of the Italian Communist party as the main opposition, the clarification may be impeded by a stalemated balance of forces. Instead, if properly employed, a fuzzy agreement has merits. Learning to live with it means giving the reasons for its fuzziness a political dignity of their own. It means recognizing the essential role of all actors, even if they entered the agreement from different perspectives, and adjusting the role to circumstances. It means calling for a degree of muddling through and accommodation in the institutional implementation of the agreement, and in performance, that makes that recognition operative. And it means making room for political minorities and the opposition—when it comes, for instance, to their control and influence upon government—that can compensate for such costs of a political stalemate as the opposition's inability to head the government. All of this is of substantial constitutional value because, given their initial subjective and objective imperfection, the agreement and its implementation invite at the same time a more demanding and continuous testing by political actors.

I have dealt at greater length with the third way of improving upon the original agreement for one good reason. Learning to live with an imperfect agreement may seem a peculiar method of improvement. Yet, more than the other ways, it reveals how pervasive and effective readiness to adjust, and to coexist in diversity, can be. This readiness, often invisible to the skeptical analyst, makes muddling through an effective fallback position when more direct and explicit ways of reworking the agreement fail. Thus, living with an imperfect agreement may not yet constitute a consensus on fundamentals, but, because it makes room for political actors with contrasting expectations, it is a useful approximation of it. Need I add that, even in some well-established democracies, what often passes for a consensus on fundamentals is, in point of fact, only an approximation?[21]

The thrust of this section, and of the entire chapter, is that reaching democratic agreement is sufficient to usher in a fruitful period of implementation and institutionalization, with all that the period holds in store for democratic stabilization. But I have asserted repeatedly that the agreement is a watershed in another sense. It is also necessary: without it, democratic institutions lead a meager existence, democratic life cannot resume in full, and in sum, to put it starkly, a democracy does not yet exist. It is time to conclude with this second aspect. Showing the cramping effects of its absence is another way of showing the potentials of a democratic agreement.

CONCLUSIONS

There have been many cases in which single democratic institutions and procedures have been adopted and tested after an authoritarian crisis but before a collective democratic agreement is struck and before breakdown games have lost significance. Some of the best examples come from Central American countries like Guatemala and El Salvador, though what I have to say might also apply to a number of countries in South America. For a number of years now, moderate forces in these countries have experimented, even in earnestness and not without bravery, with free elections, parliaments, party competition, and other standard features of political democracy. Yet the problem of the extremes, reluctant to join the democratic fray to say the least, remains unresolved, and breakdown games continue to condition democratic governance. In the absence of a collective agreement, democratic institutions are weakened by dissenters and the uncommitted and are unable to emerge as the sites for processing conflict.

The institutional feebleness of these would-be democracies has deeper historical and structural reasons, but we may also understand it contextually with regard to the circumstances that accompany and motivate the appeal to democratic institutions. Such institutions are introduced into would-be democracies, not so much to fulfill and crown a collective constitutional choice as to serve as a strategic tool, a weapon to employ, during periods of uncertainty and protracted transitions, in the contest between dissenting political forces. For example, elections ostensibly held *within* democracy are really *about* democracy. They are favored by some political actors, who call them at the sufferance or against the resistance of other actors. Assuming that democratic intentions are present, assuming that elections are revived to preempt, in a *fuite en avant,* the prejudice against coexistence and to force the issue, it is still intuitively the case that even a string of elections and a string of parliaments will find preempting the prejudice exceedingly difficult.[22]

True, we have seen earlier that calling for elections means that civilian political parties should at last emerge as the central political actors; that their attention should shift to the more orderly and constructive business of building diverse national support and defining or implementing the rules of competition; that even a prospective opposition should have an added incentive to sacrifice the support of more radical groups and reluctant players in the interest of securing wide representation from the start. All of this is eminently sensible, but it is based on an insufficiently stressed assumption. The assumption is that, in one way or another, explicitly or implicitly, willy-nilly, the significant parties have already come to an understanding, before entering the elections, that the electoral contest will offer tolerable chances of representation to all and that the newly elected body will act to constitutionalize the rules of contestation. Otherwise, if a previous understanding does not exist, the practice of elections alone has difficulties in building that understanding over time.

Chapter VIII will consider the circumstances that can nevertheless bring about, even in such difficult cases, the missing understanding—perhaps with the very help of still-marred elections. The task of these conclusions was only to reiterate the importance of reaching an understanding.

CHAPTER VII

Consolidation and Legitimacy

A Minimalist View of Two Big Words

"Consolidation" and "legitimacy" are two equally loaded and ambiguous words that, by their evocative sound, seem to hold the key to democratic success. Whereas the essay is casually littered with the latter word, and its derivatives and synonyms, the former appears rarely—the last time, gingerly, in the last chapter. Neither overuse nor avoidal comes to grips with the two terms. Now is the appropriate time to do it. Focusing on the terms is an effective means of summarizing and packaging my reflections on democratic transitions and their opportunities and strategies. Much of the task can be performed by retrieving and then weaving more tightly suggestions and strands of analysis already advanced in the essay.

The title of the chapter proclaims a minimalist view of both consolidation and legitimacy. Minimalism means that consolidation and legitimacy should not be burdened with demanding denotations because they need not be exceptional, demanding, and distant achievements—closely dependent on or connected with each other. The achievement

of consolidation does not require that a new democracy enjoy from birth rare conditions of legitimacy; nor is such rare
legitimacy the proximate product of hard-fought consolidation, without which the latter would have missed its objective. Minimalism is thus faithful not only to the theoretical
"possibilism" with which we introduced the essay but also
to the claim that democratization does not need time and
habituation.

CONSOLIDATION

In our last encounter with consolidation I suggested that this
widely used term be shorn of surfeit meaning. Consolidation
easily evokes many meanings. First of all, it can conjure up
a double process, one of which is institutionalization as defined by Samuel Huntington: "The process by which organizations and procedures acquire value and stability. The level
of institutionalization of any political system can be defined
by the adaptability, complexity, autonomy, and coherence
of its organizations and procedures."[1] From this, it is easy
to slip into another process, familiar to the reader, of socialization, through exposure and practice, to institutions and
procedures, and of development of the skills and attitudes
for dealing with them. In sum, consolidation thus construed
suggests the contemporaneous formation of both valid democratic institutions and a democratic political culture (hence
consolidation's automatic connection with the acquisition of
legitimacy).

Consolidation can easily resonate with other familiar
themes also flowing from institutionalization and socialization. It conjures up the old theme of success, failure, endurance, stability, and so forth in new democracies. It also conjures up a view of the process as lengthy: a second stage in
democratic reconstruction that begins only when democratic

institutions are set up. Finally, it evokes a view of an almost always difficult and decisive process. Rare are the new democracies in which consolidation is uneventful, short, and assured.

But my essay militates against much contained in these views. Some sociology of knowledge may assist me before I rest my case. Many students of democratization may regard it as a long and difficult process because (to return to themes treated under democratic diffusion) their critical interest has been inspired by, and indeed hostage to, the resounding and unquestionable democratic failures during the interwar period in Europe. The first captives were those generations of scholars that either witnessed the interwar years in their maturity or were formed as professionals and young adults during those years. But something of the same has happened to their disciples.

After being sidetracked briefly by the promises of decolonization and democracy in the Third World, the disciples returned to the pessimist fold. To the European lessons of the interwar period, they added those of the Third World, variously extending or reworking them to make sense of that turbulent cultural fragment of Europe that is Latin America. This generational freezing has resulted in a theoretical orientation that looks at new democracies in the twentieth century as inherently defective—in legitimacy, as well as in performance.

We thus emerge in the 1950s and 1960s with a superabundance of hypotheses and hunches—a veritable catalogue of everything that could go wrong with a new democracy—in which it is at times unclear precisely which weaknesses in the democratic record we mean to explain. The impression is often of too many factors interchangeably explaining too many things.

The overall pessimism of this theoretical orientation is

understandable, given that the true object of direct investigation by analysts of the interwar and immediate postwar periods was frequently not the onset of democracy but its demise. The fascination with explaining demise—an event that had already occurred—accounts for the tendency to see the event retrospectively as rooted in the very origins of the new democracies. Within this perspective, it is then natural to believe that a phenomenon called consolidation, with its ingredients of institutionalization and cultural development, is decisive in fulfilling or undoing democratization.

But if we reverse our perspective, if we look at democratization *prospectively* (as we have done through the essay also in reference to some topical historical cases), then the close-knit connections between birth, consolidation, and endurance/demise must often come into question. Must democracy live under the constant spell of its origins? On one side, the demise of a democracy has neither necessary nor sufficient connection with defects inherent in its birth. On the other side, we should not overplay defects. Democracy can gather sufficient resilience before its institutions and practitioners are put to the test of performance.

In addition, the initial resilience of democracy is not only a distinctive possibility but also an almost indispensable premise to the successful testing of its institutions. That is what I intended to convey in chapter 5 by stressing the decisiveness of reaching a *timely* democratic agreement: the agreement is sufficient to confer resilience. If we concur that the agreement is decisive, that leaves us two ways of employing the term *consolidation*. The matter is essentially nominalistic, and yet not pointless.

As a first possibility, we might use *consolidation* (precisely because it imparts decisiveness) to depict both the very process that leads to the agreement and its outcome. But this would be an unconventional, somehow perverse, use of the term, albeit illustrative of our position on the issue. As a process, consolidation would be the same as the transition proper, namely, the first, more unsettled and less predictable, phase of democratization. As an outcome, consolidation would close with the reaching of the agreement before the institutions and practices sanctioned by the agreement are put to work.

As a second possibility, we may more safely stay with the prevailing understanding—namely, that consolidation follows the agreement. But in this case, consolidation loses, as it should, its decisiveness. Institutionalization, habituation, and socialization begin in earnest after the agreement for the purpose of detailing and, at most, improving the agreement, but no more. Indeed, in the last chapter we have even seen a case, that of Italy, which must appear less than intuitive to scholars who look at institutional development and learning as inseparable from democratic stabilization. In Italy a degree of fuzziness and incoherence in the institutions and roles that encompass the democratic game has proved beneficial to stabilization. More interesting yet, fuzziness is more than the inert price paid by Italian politicians in order to bring reluctant players in the game; it is a political practice put with some virtue to its best use. Thus, strange as it is in the light of Huntington's definition, poor institutional coherence may give democratic institutions a peculiar value in the eyes of opposing players.

No doubt, most of us feel more comfortable with the second use of consolidation. Most of us undoubtedly also have some practical questions in mind, concerning consolidation thus understood, that may seem far more relevant than the fine points presented above. Consolidation might not be strictly decisive—an issue one may safely leave to the impractical scholar—but it certainly is very important. It is no time to relax. At what point, then, can democrats relax? At what point can we say that consolidation is over? And how do we recognize that point? These seem sensible questions. But the suggestion just advanced—that, as democratic life unfolds, there may still be virtue in keeping institutions fuzzy and incoherent—implies that there are no easy and uniform answers to the questions, and that in fact—if we take the questions seriously—they may paint us into a barren corner.

When can we relax? A sensible answer would seem to be that we can relax when certain institutional events and developments occur, or when certain records are set. But which?[2] The choice is often arbitrary, dictated more often by convenience and ease of recognition than by theory. It reveals how arguable or ad hoc, and therefore weak, is our understanding of what, precisely, consolidation as a whole is supposed to add to democracy. We may for instance use the event of peaceful rotation in government as almost fail-safe evidence that a democratic regime is here to stay. Several analysts, including me, have done it. At that point, democrats could certainly relax. Similarly, if we want to err always on the conservative side, we may protect ourselves by choosing as signals not just a single institutional event or development but a whole battery of them. The more the developments and the events, the better. But when a concept must be driven by its measuring problem, as it would be in this case, in all likelihood it means that the theoretical underpinning of the concept—what consolidation supposedly adds to democracy—is not clear.

Can we relax before, let us say, political parties rotate in government? Sometimes we can. An excellent case in point is, again, contemporary Italy, a country with a unique democratic history, whose significant events would fail to pass most conventional hard tests of consolidation. Yet arguing that Italian democracy is unconsolidated because rotation in government has thus far been impossible is, and has been for many years, both unenlightening and extravagant. Much the same can be said for Japanese democracy. Naturally, absence of rotation in these two democracies is no accident. The roots are in the drawbacks of Hirschman's "trespassing" paths to democratic development.[3] But does it have anything to do with whether or not democrats can relax?

Of course, if we are concerned with mislabeling cases like Japan and Italy, we might want to make the institutional tests of consolidation much easier, just as we make them difficult and fail-safe. This can be done easily because the tests usually rely on the repetition and cumulation of events: a number of free elections, a series of parliaments, the eventual stabilization of electoral results, the development of seniority in parliament, government, or party leadership. Repetition and cumulation are supposedly beneficial for familiar reasons, but the criticism is familiar, too. The passing of time is part of the process of consolidation. And if, in particular, the events are legally prescribed and due to occur at set intervals, the fact that they so occur seems reassuring. But how much time or how many repetitions are right? Again, without a theoretical guide, the arbitrariness of any choice is easy to see.

We have already discussed cases (Central America in particular) in which time alone—a number of elections or parliaments, or other supposedly significant institutional occurrences—is insufficient to advance consolidation; for example, elections and parliaments themselves come under attack. And we have discussed cases, by and large European, in which the peaceful repetition of similar institutional events, although crucial in detailing the rules of the game, is soon taken for granted. In these cases, it is not elections, parliaments, and so forth that secure democracy, but democracy

—the strong, winning potential of the democratic option, and its capacity to co-opt reluctant political actors—that secures the latter.

A worse procedure yet is to use public opinion rather than political institutions as a test to let democrats know when to relax. For why would we choose such a test unless we believe that the way we feel toward democracy is essential, or unless, in other words, we make legitimacy a paramount issue? But legitimacy is the second big word that the essay wishes to demystify.

LEGITIMACY

Like consolidation, the word *legitimacy* as commonly used is pregnant with meaning. It is equated with normative identification with democracy, with principled allegiance, with a democratic political culture, or with what we called a "democratic bias." But in this sense it is neither a precondition nor a necessary consequence of consolidation.[4] So democrats can relax.

Legitimacy Is Not Necessary

Followers of cognitive and behavioral psychology can offer an especially strong and clear-cut reason why democrats can relax. All suggestions that legitimacy is rooted in a democratic political culture imply a belief that people possess mind-sets, generalized predispositions to respond, deep-rooted orientations—none of which is observable in human interaction. They exist only as scholarly inventions.[5] But it is not necessary to take this extreme position in order to come to the same conclusions. Following Dankwart Rustow's lesson, we have argued from the beginning that a democratic political culture need not preexist, and in fact rarely preexists, the onset of a democratic transition. Equally, such culture need not be created, and is not likely to be created, as the transition unfolds, as a democratic agreement is reached, or as consolidation evolves. It makes sense that a democratic political culture takes time and habituation. Rustow himself, the reader may recall, suggests a time span of one generation.[6] But does this mean we cannot relax until the new generation comes of age? I believe democrats begin to relax, with good cause, much earlier.

They begin to relax when behavior is focused on crafting a democratic agreement. And when behavior is thus focused, that is all the analyst should wish to know. The fact is sufficient to inform us that consent, compliance, and support (to use terms less loaded than legitimacy) are being achieved. It informs us that the threat of breakdown games is being removed as an issue in decisions and choices during democratization. And, if instead of consent or compliance we still wish to speak of legitimacy, then let us use the term and its derivatives (loyalty, allegiance) without psychological and cultural implications.

As we have seen through the essay, political actors have many reasons to consent to democracy. In some cases they may well be motivated by a democratic bias and cultural predispositions. But in other cases, what we take for legitimacy *stricto sensu* may often be reduced, as Adam Przeworski argues, to something simpler and more concrete.[7] We have spoken of simple convenience and of other regime choices being less appealing or not available or riskier. We have spoken of political actors forced to adjust if democracy becomes the only way to treat collective interests. We have also spoken of the often decisive role of trade-offs and pacts in making democracy convenient where predispositions are weak.

We have placed special emphasis on transitions guided from the top by seceding sectors of the dictatorship (using

Spain as a particularly good case) because they illustrate most clearly why a minimalist view of legitimacy is appropriate and enlightening—why, instead, using legitimacy in the more demanding meaning as a master key to democracy is a way of narrowing or foreclosing our discoveries. Even if we momentarily assume, for instance, that the Spanish people, exposed as they had been for decades to the example and the economic influence of European democracies, were somehow already ripe for democracy, then would it not be excessive and a bit naive to claim in so few words that its authoritarian elites had become similarly converted to democracy? The statement would be unenlightening. Yet the fact remains that the decisive impetus to regime transformation came from within the regime. So, how should we understand that impetus? A realization that past ways were becoming obsolete? A calculus of the costs or uselessness of continuing repression versus the costs (or the advantages) of switching to toleration? The bandwagon effects created on foot-draggers and holdovers by the entry into a phase of consolidation? They all seem more effective ways of understanding the incremental behavior of Spain's seceding elites than the elusive, grab-bag notion of democratic legitimacy.

Nor in fact is there much greater accuracy in the notion that authoritarian elites are compelled to reconsider their methods, whatever their beliefs, because the people, if not the elites, are converting to democracy. There is no denying the role of public opinion in pushing authoritarian elites to reconsider. Still, this role does not demand widespread popular *conversion*. The evidence reported by Peter McDonough, Samuel Barnes, and Antonio López Pina, and just plain common sense, suggests in fact that widespread popular conversion is rarely the most appropriate way to describe the significant reorientations in regime attitudes that arguably occur in public opinion.[8] To say the least, we should not assume that type of conversion. The motivations for people to abandon the regime may change from case to case; but in most cases they are probably not so different from those of political elites.

Next to the old opponents of the authoritarian regime, which may very well represent a sizable sector of the population, there are still many who acquiesced to it, and many who, while abandoning ship, continue to consider the authoritarian experience valid in its historical context. But that validity is now a thing of the past. Authoritarianism has gone wrong and become dangerous. Or it has simply lost relevance. As to those who acquiesced, their passivity may have turned into a source of embarrassment, and democratic participation is a way for them to recover their self-respect.[9] Thus nostalgia and past acquiescence do not necessarily mean resistance to the emerging democratic game, as testified for instance by the scant popular support for authoritarian parties wherever transitions succeed. Presumably, nostalgia is not enough of a stir to action.[10]

Can we say in a nutshell, then, that these developments in public opinion always amount to a conversion to democratic values and practices? I would say that, often, they are only the beginning. Yet it is an important one. To repeat, a public opinion that rethinks its attitudes toward regimes past and present in the complex ways just described can still compel elites of the past regime to reconsider their options.

Our minimalist views on the place of democratic legitimacy in transitions from the top come in, in a quite timely fashion, at a moment when events in the Communist world raise the possibility of more such transitions. That transitions from communism will be, if at all, transitions from the top is more than plausible, given the key role played by the single party in running Communist states and societies. There is also little question that the role of the single party, and many more factors, will complicate matters. Pessimism, however, is checked by the realization that transitions from the top are still possible (and in some ways, as one of our scenarios has shown, more promising than others).

For one thing, we have already argued that what seems to be a big cultural obstacle (how can authoritarian/totalitarian elites ignorant and suspicious of democratic practices, conversant mostly with repression, and often raised in societies where socialization in the values of democracy has rarely or never been given a chance, turn into democratic reformers?) is not insurmountable. And recent events in Communist Poland and Hungary already seem to testify to this. Even though they are not resocialized, Communist elites, like other elites, may be driven to reform by other calculations, motivations, and mechanisms triggered by external pressures. Some of the pressures originate abroad, as we will see in the concluding chapter, but some are domestic.

Among the domestic pressures, perhaps most important is the surprising degree to which the citizens of Communist countries have resisted decades of cultural isolation and Socialist socialization, are rejecting their regimes, and are now exposed and attracted to Western life-style models. Indeed, the amazing tenacity of civil society in Eastern Europe, combined with the inability of those regimes to establish those forms of semipluralist co-optation of society that mark right-wing authoritarianism, may be such that what we will witness in Eastern Europe may be closer to that rare occurrence; namely, a veritable popular conversion to democracy.[11]

Be that as it may, the issue, in sum, is not what reforming elites, Communist or authoritarian, can or wish to hold as ultimate political values, but what they wish to and can do in response to crisis. On the latter point, the recent pragmatic concern voiced by a top Polish Communist leader is instructive: "All the textbooks tell us how difficult it is to seize power. But no one has described how difficult it is to relinquish power."[12]

But Is Legitimacy Better?

I have argued that legitimacy in the more demanding meaning is both rare and unneeded. But would it not be a significant addition? Could we answer "no" to such a question? Yet, in its candor, this is another insidious question. It hides a deceptively softer version of the notion that legitimacy is a requirement. Answering in the affirmative can inadvertently make us slide back into the vicious-circle belief that democracies born without subjective legitimacy (as most new democracies are) will both suffer in their performance and be less able to sustain that performance, and that this in turn shall delay their legitimation. But there is more that helps performance than legitimacy—and more that helps legitimacy than performance.

We can measure performance by objective, means-end efficacy and effectiveness, criteria. But performance is also in the eyes of the beholder: the same performance is perceived or evaluated differently in different countries and historical contexts. No matter. Neither aspect is really at risk because legitimacy is not yet present. We spent the previous chapter arguing that the achievement of a democratic agreement, with its immediate psychological and strategic/organizational commitments, is more decisive for both aspects. It can move government policies beyond the confining conditions of the transition while fostering among political actors fewer policy expectations and greater tolerance toward performance.

Let me add now that, even if democratic values and habits (which encourage tolerance toward performance) are not yet rooted, other and more readily available external factors can offer succor. I will recall two of them because they are of special help in contemporary transitions. One is the absence of attractive regime alternatives capable of offering comprehensive worldviews to supplant democracy. At times when, as during the interwar period and following World War II, dictatorships of the left and right exercised wide popular appeal, at times when democracy was on the defensive, the performance of many democracies appeared, to many predisposed beholders, to be failing. The ideology of regeneration proffered by the extreme right and left—and for that matter the appeal of newfangled state interventionism to democrats themselves—put democratic performance to a serious test. In other words, the crisis of some democracies during such periods of defiance was not just one of objective performance. Displeasure with performance was greater not necessarily where performance was objectively poorer, but where alternative regime models had made, for other reasons, greater domestic inroads.[13]

Today, however, the alternative models are gone or discredited, perhaps nowhere more than where they are still practiced. And just as this helps to route incipient authoritarian crises in a democratic direction and assists the transfer of support, so also, once democratic governments have been established, it sustains their credibility as they begin to struggle with problems of governance. That is why the same crisis of performance may have different effects on different democracies or at different historical conjunctures. That is why we should be wary of drawing quick analogies between crises.

Almost identical points can be made—and we need only recall them—for the second, related external factor that influences present responses to performance. As alternative regime models fade, so also the level of expectations about what democracy can and should deliver has decreased. It is better to say that, though it is no longer the harbinger of instant material progress, democracy has gained dramatically for delivering something else: mutual security in diversity.[14] Here is where democracy holds the unmistakable advantage; witness the resistance that Communist regimes are meeting when they try to circumvent civic/political reforms by emphasizing economic ones and by insulating the latter from the former.[15] When it comes to democratic performance, material policies usually associated with it are not the only ones, or indeed the first ones, to count. Poor material performance can be offset by civic/political conquests.

We have inadvertently come full circle. For if material performance is not the only criterion by which we judge, if civic-political reforms acquire a paramount value in guiding and softening reactions to material performance, then the bases on which we come to accept democracy reveal themselves to be broader and sturdier. Poor material performance does not necessarily hamper the building of democratic support, nor does it hinder the development, in the longer run, of a democratic political culture—no more than the initial weakness of the democratic culture hampers performance and its popular reception.[16]

But to be able to distinguish empirically between people's support for democracy and people's perception of material performance clarifies concrete situations only up to a point. It is still difficult for scholars and analysts in the field to orient themselves in the maze of signals that come from public reactions to democratic performance. Their disorderliness often overwhelms us. Hence some additional cautionary notes are in order before we draw conclusions about material performance and legitimacy. Citizens react not only to government policies but also to collective outcomes, economic trends, turns of events, and so forth that, strictly speaking, are not the result of government choices. Are they holding government responsible for the latter as well? They frequently are—

though not always.[17] And if they are, what aspect of government are they holding responsible? If displeasure it is, then displeasure at what?

Not all public displeasure is directed at the regime but may be part, like partisan approval, of the democratic game wherein all sorts of accusations are hurled against governments and their presumed policy mistakes. Among the accusers may be incurable nostalgics, disappointed democrats, or electoral competitors for popular support. It is equally part of the game that government sympathizers will appropriate successes, achievements, lucky turns of events, and favorable opinion climates that are not always of the government's making.

Nor should we see displeasure as sufficient evidence that a new democracy, by being new and untried, suffers from inherent problems of governance. In most contemporary transitions, problems of governance in the material sphere reflect not only the inheritance from past regime policies and particularly weak economies but also the international conjuncture. As for the latter, new and older democracies share a common plight. Do citizens know the difference? Do we? More important, do we know and care whether citizens know the difference?

Finally, not every poor performance, whether measured objectively or by public reactions, sets off a spiral of more poor performances, leading eventually to a regime crisis. Take for example the not-so-new southern European democracies of the mid-1970s (Latin America is too early to call). None of them has been a paragon of uniformly successful material performance. Even in Spain, where economic growth has been quite sustained, people face two-digit unemployment and the social conservatism of the Socialist government. Evidence also suggests a growing popular concern with economic performance, captured by such self-mocking quips as Spain's "against Franco, we lived better" and a novel readiness to take governments and parties to task.[18] But there is no evidence of an accompanying fall in regime support or of escalating and tunnel effects. All of this means that, once the democratic game has been secured, material performance can become, to be sure, a relevant and even paramount public opinion issue. But it does so precisely against a more vigorous background of agreed-upon democratic rights and practices that are not necessarily hampered by the open concern and conflict over performance that they positively sanction and invite.

CONCLUSIONS

More than conclusions, the considerations that follow are prolegomena to the following chapter.

By debunking consolidation and legitimacy, the essay justifies its thesis that political democratization should not be rightfully seen as a prolonged affair. Quite to the contrary, when matters get prolonged, we would be better advised to worry. Everything suggests that matters get prolonged not because democracy needs time but because democratization has met some hefty stumbling blocks. On these blocks, the very achievement of a democratic agreement stumbles. The result is something more serious than an anemic political democracy that needs fresh blood to thrive. In our vocabulary, an anemic democracy still implies a democratic agreement of sorts. In this chapter we have restated why an anemic democracy may still be capable of producing its own new blood. Thus the affliction has not been of much concern in the essay. But when—more disquietingly—the democratic agreement is itself at issue, we find ourselves locked in a kind of halfway house. Hardly a home or a shelter, this house has been labeled either a *democradura* or a *dicta-*

blanda, depending on how the materials of dictatorship and democracy, repression and liberalization, mix in its construction.

To appreciate that at issue in these halfway houses is not the incompleteness of democratic consolidation but a more basic resistance to the democratic agreement, we may recollect what is old in the house and how subordinate or confined the place of the new democratic features is. *Dictablandas* are still noncompetitive dictatorships in which a degree of bland liberalization has been used to justify the status quo.[19] They reflect the fact that institutional forces that define the dictatorship, usually the military or the single party, cannot find, invent, or negotiate novel institutional ways of operating within a dominant competitive system. They do not know how to relinquish power. Taiwan, the Soviet Union under Gorbachev, Chile as General Pinochet prepared the regime for the 1988 referendum, and Nicaragua after subscribing to the regional plan of the five Central American presidents are all cases in point.[20]

Democraduras go a step further and, in contrast to *dictablandas,* allow after a fashion a competitive system. But competition is limited in three ways by fairly explicit or formal pacts. Participation is restricted to usually conservative forces that exclude others; these forces share government offices according to consociational arrangements fairly independent of electoral verdicts; they also leave touchy issues out of the policy agenda. These arrangements reflect distrust by prominent social and corporate forces in the immediate capacity either of democracy to guarantee mutual security, or of security to guarantee their own survival. Uruguay, and Venezuela after the 1958 pact, are cases in point.

But even if a country has gone beyond *dictablanda* and *democradura* proper, some of the same restrictions may still operate, revealing that no democratic agreement is yet in sight. Civilian politics may have been able to break loose from direct supervision by the institutions of the dictatorship. It may in fact be fairly competitive and free of exclusionary pacts, at least sufficiently so (Brazil) that we may not even speak of a *democradura*. But civilian politics may still be unable to control the past: unable to control institutions of the dictatorship such as the military, possibly unable to control corporate social interests not averse to supporting those institutions. A sort of duality of power exists —at times more antagonistic, at times tolerated by civilian forces. We tentatively cited Argentina, and we may add Brazil. We should add with greater confidence—given the way we described them—El Savador, and Guatemala under President Vinicio Cerezo. But these are only examples, and the impasse of the duality is also common to other would-be democracies.

Nor should we finally forget the possibility, illustrated in our third scenario, that such hybrids—*democraduras* that might slide back, if unchecked, into a *dictablanda*—may develop not because of resistance from the old regime, but because of a situation much like Portugal's in the first two years of its transition wherein the opposition clashes internally over the nature of the new regime.

These conclusions restate the importance of the democratic agreement by illustrating the meaning of its absence. But, for all the confidence we have placed in the future of democratic life once political actors are induced to enter into an agreement, there are many ways that actors may miss the agreement and hold democracy back. There are also many halfway houses presently around. And because the global prospects for starting new democracies, rather than the prospects for preserving them once they are started, were the opening theme of this essay, this is the theme to which we return in the next chapter. Are the prospects so poor? Can dwellers move out of halfway houses?

CHAPTER VIII

To Craft Which Democracies?

This essay has been devoted to possibilism and to crafting. I wish to take the two one final step. To be sure, "possibilism" does not mean that democracy is the only possible outcome in the crisis of a dictatorship, or even the one that is generally favored. It simply means that, for all the reasons advanced in this essay, democracy can be crafted to be attractive. Besides, it would be foolhardy to deny that democratic prospects vary from case to case. In making reference to concrete cases, we have repeatedly contrasted countries where the crafting of a democratic agreement has proved difficult to countries where this has been less difficult. We have repeatedly advanced explanations for the difference. And even when we favored explanations that focus on the transition and its strategies, these in turn have begged for their own explanations—often of a deeper historical and structural nature. Similarly, we speculated about the chances of future democratization in different types of regimes and crises.

I wish to conclude this essay by revisiting the issue of whether crafting helps, even in difficult cases, to increase the number of successful transitions. After all, we should not forget that in many cases the outcome of regime crises may be sufficiently indeterminate (by being, for example, stalemated) to give crafting greater leeway. Even where prospects are bleak indeed, it is not out of order to take a second look at the outer borders of what is possible and plausible.

The essay thus closes with a bottom-line argument that proceeds as follows. The society and history of some countries, or much more so their regime and system of political domination, may make their democratic prospects less promising. Thus political halfway houses may seem more likely. But their crisis may be such that status quo options are drastically curtailed and halfway houses may themselves represent costly impasses. This is where the subjective expediency of crafting can provide succor. In the process it may also dull the theoretical shine about "objective" democratic prospects.

In 1984 Samuel Huntington, whose observations on the global prospects of democracy offered the first foil to my reflections, wrote that the prospects are bleak.[1] But in 1989 Zbigniew Brzezinski, writing about particularly nasty and tenacious dictatorships, announced in no uncertain terms: "It is almost a certainty that at some point in the relatively near future, given some major economic or political upheaval, politics as the expression of authentic social aspirations for multiparty democracy will truly return to the life of Eastern Europe."[2] Numerically, the prospect of some Communist countries going democratic may not subtract much from Huntington's accounting; but it does raise questions about some tenets of development theory. Bearing on the latter, Huntington offered two independent explanations why "the likelihood of democratic development in Eastern Europe is virtually nil."[3] One is the Soviet veto, and the other is that Communist systems, even when drifting from totalitarianism toward authoritarianism, cannot renounce in principle their political control of the economy.[4]

Given these discrepant assessments, it appears that some old certainties no longer hold. At the end of the 1970s Jeane Kirkpatrick gained public attention by pointing to a commonly held ultimate distinction between authoritarian and totalitarian regimes: the former, but not the latter, can be replaced.[5] Now totalitarianism has been prefixed with a tantalizing "post," and Brzezinski doubts whether that significant distinction is still unshakable. If the prospects for democracy in tenacious Communist regimes can be reconsidered, why not reconsider prudently the prospects in other, and otherwise difficult, regimes? Where should prudence draw the bottom line?

What follows is not a complete account intended to review by cases and types democratic prospects worldwide. We are content to take a narrower, most-difficult-case approach, focused on the study of selected regimes. If we can show that indeterminacy and crafting still have room where, given the stubborn nature of particular regimes, the prospects are bleak, we can then make a stronger claim where the prospects are better. A source of confidence in the general prospects for democracy comes from the realization that most contemporary nondemocratic regimes should eventually experience crises stemming largely from betrayed expectations about their material performance.[6] A source, on the other hand, of soberness comes from a theme familiar to the essay: today's crises should neither plainly topple the regimes and their personnel, nor induce the regimes, if the matter depended on them alone, to accept full political democracy.

Naturally, however, matters rarely if ever depend exclusively on regimes and their ingrained preferences. Let me thus test two types of regimes that, for different reasons, are uncommonly resilient or, when not unmistakably routed and overthrown, singularly resistant to accepting full change. Is their resistance unshakable?

TESTING RESILIENT REGIMES

The two types ostensibly find themselves at the opposite ends of the spectrum of contemporary dictatorships. The first one is the traditional authoritarianism, infused with sultanism and personalism, that characterizes countries in the Middle East, North Africa, and Central America. I will sample out of this group the authoritarian regimes of Central America, whose military nature distinguishes them for favoring violent exists from their crises of political domination. The other type is Communist totalitarianism, whose personalism and traditionalism, though not always insignificant (North Korea, Romania, and China being only the most blatant examples), are supposedly cast within or superseded by the impersonal, pervasive, systematic, and mobilizational rule of the single party.[7]

Let us begin with Central America. We have already contrasted the Western European with the Central American experience to point out why the respective dictatorships made exit toward democracy a likely occurrence in the former (even irrespective, for the countries that returned to democracy immediately after World War II, of its effects) but makes it a more distant one in the latter.[8]

West European dictatorships had to contend with a number of state/political institutions with histories of their own, as professional carriers of public functions, that predated the advent of dictatorship. Efforts to uproot or radically politicize these institutions (bureaucracies, armies, judiciaries) were limited and halfhearted, or resulted in failure, or, once the dictatorships faced their crisis, revealed themselves as ephemeral. As a rule, the institutions were expressly incorporated by the dictatorships to parallel new and specifically repressive or totalitarian institutions. The effect, not always or completely unintentional, was to restrain the regime's totalitarian features. In only one case (Germany) were the older institutions more clearly subordinated to the new ones. But, whatever their new place, the old state institutions never became coterminous with or were defined by dictatorship.[9] Thus, at the moment of crisis the institutional weight of the past (a liberal and even democratic past) was central in helping European countries return to competitive politics. Not only could the structure of the state be more easily recycled to serve democracy, but also state institutions had an interest of their own in separating from dictatorship and being recycled, thus taking a step toward reaffirming their professional autonomy.

By contrast, the state institutions of the Central American countries that have experienced dictatorship are not just hostages or morose partners of their regimes. In countries where the state lacks a tradition of autonomy and impersonality, but shows one of primitive parasitism, in countries where public functions are privatized and the state operates intermittently,[10] it can be said instead (though the expression unduly suggests the impossibility of change) that state institutions have a "natural affinity" for a form of dictatorship that is itself parasitic and predatory, and in which depredation is both personalistic and militarily organized.[11] Why then should such state institutions, coterminous with dictatorship, be interested in recycling themselves for democracy? As we saw when discussing trade-offs, democracy has no immediate trade-offs to offer them and would instead threaten the logic of patrimonial appropriation by which they live. Why should a military, which in the region uses the state as both object and agent of violent appropriation, renounce its privileged arrangement? Military leaders of Central America have a personalized praetorian conception of the state and of the relations they (as men of arms) have with their own military institution that is a far cry from that of, say, the Spanish military, whose reasons for installing the Spanish dictatorship had quite different roots. Thus it would seem that only a violent overthrow, not a negotiated transition, could dislodge similar regimes. Indeed, it is difficult to see how their opponents can place much trust, or rally much interest, in the willingness of the regimes to reform themselves.

A similar lack of interest in a negotiated transition characterizes in principle Communist regimes. The essay is laced with numerous, provisional, statements to this effect, but the essential point is simple, and not dissimilar to one of Huntington's points. It emerges quite well in the canonical contrast between communism and the also ambitious Fascist or semi-Fascist regimes of Western Europe. Despite fascism's ambition, communism, much more than fascism, is the master of a political program that, upon taking over the state, subjects state institutions to total guidance. Even when systematic terror subsides, the guidance does not lack justification. Indeed, by collectivizing the economy, Communist *nomenklaturas,* more clearly than their Fascist counterparts, build a doctrinally justified vested interest in their own survival. This holds them together and stymies lateral secessions.

Secessions are similarly stymied because a collectivized economy does not tolerate the survival and operation of influential corporate/economic interests—the type of interests (such as labor, professional, or business associations) that would be likely to look at their probable alliance with the regime as one of convenience and to act accordingly when the convenience fades. In fact, totalitarian disruption of collective bonds supposedly travels beyond state and corporate interests to reach civil society at large and therefore the innumerable horizontal and often primary ties that allow people to act together.

Thus, it would follow from this model of communism that only limited reforms from the very core of the regime are conceivable, if at all. Further, Communist regimes have no reasons or no capacity to push reforms that jeopardize their *nomenklaturas*. Conversely, if the regime is interested only in limited reforms, civil society may not put much trust in those reforms and may lack the capacity (and possibly the interest) to obtain more.

If we now put the two models side by side—the Communist model and that of Central American despotism—we may understand the skepticism about how far their transformation can go. The fact that a number of Communist regimes settle for a sort of *dictablanda* should not imply their demise. There is similarly an impasse in Central America, where Panama is an embattled dictatorship, Guatemala and El Salvador have taken the road to democracy but cannot rein in military violence, and Honduras suffers from the same problem to a lesser degree. But we should not expect that impasses must somehow come to a felicitous end. For, in both cases, the models of dictatorship offer ample reasons to doubt foreseeable breakthroughs.

Yet excessive dependence on the models can also paint us into an intellectual corner. Both models imply that—because the leadership of the respective regimes, whether the regimes are still in existence or have been recently set aside, see no appealing trade-offs in the democratic compromise—stalling, repression, breakdown games, even military violence are therefore still among the methods that, each fitting its own circumstances, presumably pay off. The problem, then, is what to make, for instance, of the following statement issued by the leader of the Communist group in the Polish lower house after voting for the election of a Solidarity prime minister: "Perhaps, we and our honorable colleagues from Solidarity had to live through tough years and mature separately before meeting. As to my party, *maybe it was necessary to end up with our back to the wall for us to understand reality*." [12]

But the answer to the problem (why does the regime not resist?), an answer that can take us out of the intellectual corner, is starkly contained in the statement itself: Assumptions to the contrary notwithstanding, resistance may indeed no longer pay off. It may no longer pay off in Communist regimes and in other regimes as well. It is not, in other words, unshakably true that our regimes are impervious to change, despite the way they have been canonically depicted. They may lose in the most incontrovertible way—on their own terms, because their methods do not achieve their goals. And when this happens, a new way may emerge of looking at the costs of toleration versus those of resistance and repression. Toleration may still seem costly, but if resisting change turns out, by its total ineffectiveness, to be incomparably more costly, then toleration may invite a second look. This is another way of understanding Robert Dahl's axiom about repression and toleration.

We should point out that a stalemate between regime and opposition is not the ultimate predicament it seems to be. Stalemates are by no means unusual ways of setting transitions in motion, but resemble what Dankwart Rustow believes to be the lever of democratic transitions: an inconclusive struggle, the protracted ineffectiveness of resistance, weariness, and disillusion; all of which makes outcomes indeterminate and may thus lead to final shifts in the strategies and even objectives of political actors. [13]

The fact that a stalemate forces some of the regimes we

are focusing on to seek collective exits out of the stalemate raises serious questions, especially in the case of Communist regimes, about the value of our canonical models. Under the Communist model, a stalemate or, more so, an old regime's willingness to seek an exit that could travel all the way to democracy seem well-nigh inconceivable. If it turns out to be conceivable, this is only partly because, understandably, the model of a steady regime does not concern itself with crisis, demise, and strategic responses to them. Another and more important reason may well be that the model over-states the tightness, overbearing presence, pervasiveness, and therefore resilience of the mechanisms for regime domina-tion.[14] It may also be, as part of the latter problem, that the model (a handy guide through reality) is one matter and the realities another.[15] In the first place, the model does not ap-ply equally well to all concrete regimes. When it comes, for instance, to the pervasiveness and penetration of the Com-munist totalitarian model and its fit in concrete cases, the Soviet Union is one thing, but the often internally imported regimes of Eastern and east-central Europe are another. Yet another is China and its own domestic version of commu-nism. Thus, without by any means having exhausted the list of Communist or pseudo-Communist regimes around the world—in Asia, Africa, and Latin America—we already have our hands filled with different possibilities and trends, as students of Communist models are well aware.

But picking at models and paradigms is neither my final assignment nor my forte. My final assignment is to explore the full value of a stalemate as a first step out of the most stubborn regimes; to show how an otherwise unlikely dem-ocratic exit may be brought about by a situation in which the divergent interests of stubborn actors can be satisfied jointly or (stalemate) not at all; to see how crafting may insert itself in the situation to produce joint satisfaction. Let me carry the assignment one more step by examining how, when resistance becomes nonproductive, our two types of regimes may be forced and then enticed to reconsider their behavior. The exercise will also serve to remind us that recognizing and exploiting the appropriate conditions for a democratic exit may fall victim to human misperception and miscalculation. Therefore, optimism about the future boundaries of democracy should always be tempered by prudence.

Exiting from Central American Regimes

As to Central America, the important note of prudence is that weariness, growing from the realization that resistance and violence no longer pay, may be long in coming. The recent state of affairs in the region should suggest weariness, yet signs of readiness for a collective exit from the impasse are unclear. A predatory military with no institutional affinity for democracy may feel for a long time that it has nothing to lose by persevering with violence, even as its material returns, so crucial to the military, may stagnate, even as violence achieves no rollback. The military may therefore put up with a protracted struggle, which gets further protracted by radical armed resistance on the other side. Thus, in a region where, in addition, civil society is too thin and political formations are too poorly implanted to impose by themselves a process of peaceful reconstruction of collective life—in a region where revolt against repression, violence in response to violence, are endemic political currency—violence may as easily flare up as subside and weariness may as easily dissipate.

Still, nothing we have said declares weariness to be unproductive. Rather, the point to be stressed in relation to Central America is that, if weariness must break the spiral of violence, special timing is necessary to take advantage of it before it dissipates. Because weariness is also relative (in-effective strategies become tiresome as concrete alternatives surface), it is also necessary that a concrete political settle-ment be proffered at the moment of weariness, perhaps by third parties. This may well be the only way to break the spiral in a peaceful manner. Thus, the theme of pacts re-appears.

When first discussing pacts, we argued that in Central America there is nothing to trade off—except, we may now interject, when weariness sets in. We have similarly seen, when discussing elections as a lever for democratization, why unilaterally called elections are a weak weapon to persuade actors engaged in breakdown games to abandon their resis-tance. This is because such elections are not instruments for trade-offs. They do not constitute the type of political settle-ment that guarantees who plays what roles, which the re-gion preliminarily needs. We may now interject, however, that in the presence of weariness, elections may serve to nudge political actors from resistance toward settlement. Elections become a more useful weapon. The ability of moderate po-litical actors to run fairly competitive elections and to get out the votes during stalemated violence (and both words need emphasis) is per se an achievement with a potential to co-opt dissident actors that should not be discounted.[16] The examples of El Salvador and Guatemala come to mind, but we may also draw a lesson from Portugal.[17]

To be sure, the new democratic institutions of Portugal were not as weak as those of Central America. Still, two regime projects, as we saw them, confronted each other: one by the civil-military left and the other by the moderate par-ties. As a result, democratic institutions were introduced at the sufferance of the left, the constitution was emerging as something other than a full democratic compromise, and elections were dismissed by the left. Nonetheless, what began to break the developing stalemate and cracked the cohesion of the left by showing a failure in its strategies was the very ability of the moderate parties to use the elections effectively as a weapon against their detractors and to compel them to come finally to terms with political democracy.

But the Portuguese case offers Central America another lesson: that of the importance of negotiated exits. Finding a constitutional settlement satisfactory to all Portuguese, while removing from the settlement what the left originally aspired to, has taken political realignments, painstaking caution, and careful transactions—occasionally stronger tactics notwithstanding. In the more difficult Central American context, a careful political settlement is not only equally necessary but also, unlike Portugal, cannot wait for the ineffectiveness of violence to become glaring on its own. It bears emphasis that in order to expose its ineffectiveness, violence should be challenged by its alternative, as it is, in fact, challenged in the regional settlement proposed by the five Central American presidents.[18] Further, settlements cannot but be formally negotiated. Unspoken concessions, temporary withdrawals, implicit accommodations, ambiguous muddling through would exercise limited attraction by leaving in doubt the nature of the democratic game and the place of the contestants.

Last in treatment, but first in importance remains the question of what precisely a predatory military that must be negotiated out of its instinctive preferences (other avenues being closed by the stalemate) can obtain in exchange for unchallenged civilian rule. Once more, the answer is stark. It can obtain what, under normal circumstances, it has never been interested in. It can obtain its survival in a radically altered institutional form: that of a professional military, carrying explicitly assigned public functions. Thus, in order to break the spiral of violence, a negotiated settlement must contain not only an electoral pact (of importance especially, though not exclusively, for the armed opposition) but also measures that would pursue what European polities had fortunately achieved before their authoritarian interlude; that is, the depersonalization of armies and other legal institutions of the state.

In the southern hemisphere, where professionalism has been equated with counterinsurgent ideologies of national security and with views of the military as the irreplaceable institutional guarantor of the constitutional order, professionalism is often taken to be the problem rather than the solution. Nevertheless, a professional military, more than a predatory or praetorian one, can be rooted in, and protected by, corporate guarantees that alleviate its need to dominate politics and society. Also, the prospects of a professional military may still seem slight. Yet, we must remember that conversions do not happen en masse and all at once, but through bandwagon effects.

As the psychology of secessions shows, blocs come apart progressively, revealing that even the most cohesive institutions are never perfectly so, but incorporate clusters of interests that respond differently to internal crises and external solicitations. If this is true of institutions with a collective public function, it may in one special way be even truer in our case. If a military with limited professionalization fails in its chief task—the effective perpetration of domestic violence—there is little else to hold it together. Thus, few situations work better than a protracted stalemate (if exploited at the right time) in dividing such a military. In addition, if the chief object of military violence—i.e., armed civilian resistance—is also included in a general settlement, military cohesiveness has even less reason to endure.

Besides, a perfect predatory and praetorian military—totally insensitive to alternative roles, totally in command of the society that is the object of its depredation, totally tied to equally parasitic civilian oligarchies—does not exist in reality. Our attention to regime models should not blind us to the fact that in specific countries and specific historical contexts sectors of the military in the southern hemisphere have been tempted by more dignified roles, or that the alliance of the military with civilian oligarchies has occasionally come apart.[19]

We should nurture no excessive expectations about the democracies that might emerge from the political settlements being sought today in Central America. The settlements may give birth to democracies where the military's role is still a matter of concern; where political parties run the gamut from *personalismo* to clientelism, populism and Third World radicalism, pay lip-service to or shelter myths about social revolution, and embrace chauvinist and anti-imperialist creeds; and where all the while social transformations go unattended. Nonetheless, such democracies would be an unquestionably positive change—not just because they would disprove scholarly pessimism, but because they would be infinitely superior to anything their people now have.

Finally—although the Central American model is not appropriate for understanding the regime preferences of South American civilian and military institutions—Central America (and perhaps more so Portugal) contains some strategic lessons for the new South American democracies, where the status of the democratic agreement is ambiguous. A disturbing sign in South America comes from the contingent difficulties with adjusting state and corporate interests to democracy, and therefore from the lack of pacts in regional transitions. In the region's embattled democracies, moderate forces may have to fall back on a battle of attrition, in which democratic institutions with a capacity for mass appeals are employed, as they were in Portugal, to wear down resistance. But, with enfeebled institutions, attrition and stronger tactics alone should be last resorts. By themselves, without accompanying evidence that the democratic agreement pays, they may be insufficient for the task—leaving our democracies where they are now, at best. In Dahl's axiom, the costs of responding to democracy with repression are also a function of what democratic cooperation can offer instead.

Exiting from Communist Regimes

What is there for a Communist regime to trade off? I will approach the answer from a distance by bringing out one point of contrast between Communist and right-wing authoritarian regimes. It may be true that the latter are less durable than the former. But, at least in the Central American context, the lesser longevity does not stem from some greater propensity of authoritarian regimes to reform themselves slowly. Rather, when they are not stubbornly resisting, their inclination has been to step down abruptly, albeit often temporarily, to avoid dealing with untreatable emerging situations. In keeping with this mode of extrication, what accompanied the extrication was, not a series of reforms initiated by the regimes, but the strained resumption of competitive practices and institutions (elections, parties, unions, parliaments, civic and local associations) that the regimes had repressed or made a mockery of, but had rarely if ever formally abolished. Recent events in some Communist countries reveal instead no stepping down, but a flurry of reforms by Communist leaders. The reforms come on the heels of, but also go well beyond, a much more limited and often reversed history of reforms dating back to the beginnings of post-totalitarianism.

One way of understanding the difference is to note that the Central (and South) American pendulum between authoritarian and pluralist regimes—with the military largely deciding when to step in or out—is patently inconceivable in Communist regimes. Communism is not a temporary caretaking affair, a *régime d'exception* with a limited, self-imposed mandate to put a disrupted or disrupting democratic house in order, as many authoritarian regimes like to present/disguise/justify themselves. Communism's original ambition is to offer, socially and politically, a permanent alternative, not just domestic but above all global, to liberal democracy. In turn, this very ambition may paradoxically explain Communist reforms when the ambition carries risks. At such points, reforms are judged essential for Communist survival.

A basic qualitative distinction must, however, be drawn between the earlier Communist reforms and the present ones. Only the latter ones carry a real, if unanticipated or unavoidable, potential for breaking up the unity of Communist *nomenklaturas* and eroding their centrality. Thus, only the latter ones create open-ended conditions for internal disagreement on the extent to which communism should be transformed. The reason for the distinction is that all earlier reforms remained within communism's pristine ambition to replace democracy the world over. In fact, they served to rescue the ambition, against domestic resistance and international obstacles. Recent reforms, on the contrary, are designed to rescue domestic Communist regimes from that very ambition and to set it aside—as the ambition appears finally unviable, except at internal costs that neither stonewalling nor retrenching regimentation can reverse.

In other words, present reforms and their potential for eroding Communist apparats reflect the fact that for the first time the global objective for which, and the global context within which, communism came to power, kept itself in power, socialized its economies, and entrusted them to its apparats, have both ceased to hold. In essence, as it loses international coherence, communism (especially outside the Soviet Union) is becoming more like other, domestically oriented, dictatorships. And the general lesson is that, unless we take into clear account these mutations and their international referents, we may lose sight of how far Communist transformations may now go.[20]

As Andrew Janos describes it, the original "focus of communism was external rather than internal, for its purpose was not 'catching up' with the advanced nations, but to destroy a modern world economy that was seemingly reproducing a pattern of debilitating economic disparities."[21] Thus the Communist dictatorships of the Soviet Union, China, and Eastern Europe were not simply developmental dictatorships each designed to close the gap of its own backwardness, but the collective harbingers and instruments of a new international order. Moreover, this global purpose, thanks to substantial tactical adaptations to permanent obstacles and changing circumstances, had in fact remained basic to communism until the first part of the 1980s. Though Stalin rejected Trotsky's vision of a global revolution through popular uprisings, global Soviet hegemony through more conventional statecraft and expansionism was still his central objective. The postwar acquisition of Eastern Europe rallied those countries to that objective. And Chinese communism, also a postwar phenomenon, displayed, in its very rift with the U.S.S.R., a similar global dedication to peasant revolutions against the "Western City." Nor did the death of Stalin signify an abandonment of the global objective, but rather a retrenchment to consolidate—under the banner of peaceful coexistence—communism's global challenge to the West. In point of fact, this relative retrenchment did not and could not go without a continuous war of attrition to sustain and test the challenge in various peripheries of the world.

Thus, what I have labeled post-totalitarian reforms were

in effect institutional adjustments to tactical shifts in a global objective. Even in Eastern Europe, where the end of Stalinism allowed some of the local Communist regimes to pay greater attention to the problem of their domestic economic performances, Brezhnev's doctrine of limited sovereignty brought brutally home the permanent superiority of the global objective.[22] And as long as this has been the case, as long as communism's socialized economies have been functional to the global objective, the integrity and indispensability of the apparats in charge of the economies have also stayed unchallenged. In fact, post-totalitarianism removed lingering menaces to party and bureaucratic integrity, security, and status that stemmed from Stalin's extralegal despotism,[23] or from the populist subversion practiced by Mao during the Cultural Revolution. Thus, in a way, it is precisely when the global objective of communism became routinized that the apparats' staying power reached its peak.

But party and bureaucratic integrity lost much of its endurance and *raison d'être* when—after Brezhnev in the Soviet Union and Mao in China—the global objective receded, making room in the Soviet Union, Eastern Europe, and China for more routine concerns with domestic backwardness and development. According to prevailing analyses, this momentous shift may be explained by the devastating drain made by socialized economies on domestic resources, worsened when the economies had to be geared primarily to sustain the global objective. The inability of socialized economies to carry domestic growth, let alone the global objective, and the great deprivations that this state of affairs has cost Communist societies, reached crisis proportions as Communist societies became more exposed to Western political and lifestyle models, and as the price tag for maintaining global parity with the West became unbearable.

Thus, neither the more recent lowering of existing barriers to communication and exchange between East and West nor the post-totalitarian emergence of an implicit "social contract" between Communist governments and their societies, could reabsorb the crisis.[24] On the contrary, by their timidity, these socially ameliorative steps, when consciously compared to their Western counterparts, both announced and intensified the crisis. We should make no mistake. In regimes that, for all their retrenchment from goals, still attach tremendous importance to a historical and popular mission, the protracted failure to rally a sullen population to new but still less than believable performance goals signifies a major dispiriting setback.

Whatever the reasons for the crisis, the fact that the global objective has receded and that growth and social issues have become central and yet most difficult to treat, signifies, as anticipated, that present Communist *nomenklaturas* have become dysfunctional: no longer the solution, they are now the problem. Thus, their cohesiveness and monopoly of power, which are so much part of the functioning totalitarian model (and, in some ways, even more of the post-totalitarian one), are seriously shaken by reforms. For reforms that touch upon the political classes now reflect and demand not adjustment but a shift in the objectives—for which *nomenklaturas* are hardly equipped. It follows that reforms undermine the vertical and horizontal coherence of the political classes. If the latter rally against reforms, as the conventional view has it, loyalty to the leadership comes into question. And if reforms trigger latent, and previously less consequential, horizontal differences—tied to specific institutional functions—the ability to give reformed communism a reconstituted administrative backbone comes into question.

To be sure, the core leadership (from which, and only from which, change originates) wishes reforms but also wishes to save the political class, no matter how transformed and trimmed. But it is hardly clear to anybody how the double feat should be achieved because of the unprecedented shift in goals and reforms and the inseparability of socioeconomic and institutional reforms. At what point do reforms intended both to revitalize society and save its political class instead contribute to the latter's disunity and even demise? If, in addition, civil society resurfaces, as it has in many Communist countries, with a decisiveness that takes the political classes by surprise, communism is faced with previously untested dilemmas on how far to proceed, if at all.

Communist leaders have given different responses to the dilemmas. But in all cases their responses have proved incapable of reabsorbing the crisis of their political classes. We may distinguish two types of responses. In the first one, exemplified by China, leaders may give precedence to the new objective of economic development through more market-oriented policies while keeping a tight political lid on civil society (and on the political class). In this way, the unity and centrality of the political class should presumably be reconstituted around a core that is politically conservative yet institutionally in charge of economic reforms within a political command context, and all the while shielded from civil society. In point of fact, however, backing away from political liberalization and trying in other ways (stern if necessary) to reconstitute the loyalty and unity of the political class appear to be only troublesome stopgap measures hiding unresolved tensions within the class—tensions that both reflect and intensify those in civil society.[25]

The second (Soviet and Eastern European) response fares no better at reconstituting a shaken political class and may instead accelerate its visible coming apart. At the same time, it has a potential of its own for inducting a Communist class, wholly or in part, and willy-nilly, into competitive politics.

The second response consists in going precisely in the opposite direction to the first by giving priority to a modicum of politico-institutional liberalization. It does so in order to sell difficult economic reforms that will, if adopted, have a high cost for Communist societies.[26] The response relies on a closer rapport between reforming leaders and civil society. As in other transformations of dictatorship that are guided from the top, reformers calculate that the revival of civil society, stimulated by the very transformations in regime performance and purposes and by international demonstration effects, is irreversible beyond a certain point. They thus use such revival, and in part direct and favor it, to pressure reluctant political classes into supporting limited reforms. Still, support may not be easy to gain. Reforms may instead change institutional roles and thereby introduce conflict among them.

With a leadership pushing for some institutional diversification and divestment in a context of political liberalization, and with a political class now unable or unwilling to resummon communism's global purpose without fostering (especially in Eastern Europe) further institutional divisions, the unity of the political class may now be as threatened as that of its counterparts in other *dictablandas* similarly perched between past and future. As in the case of the other *dictablandas,* its unity (and in fact the unity of the leadership) behind limited reforms intended to prevent collapse becomes contingent on the credibility of that intent—an intent that is already shaken by institutional diversification and divestment. Indeed, measures to decentralize public tasks, to divest institutions of excessive powers, to create new bodies for legal or public control—all to loosen the stranglehold of *nomenklaturas* and revive performance—seriously test the vertical and horizontal solidarity of the political class. With what consequences for class behavior?

One possibility is an increase in class fears of being placed at risk, or even jettisoned, by reforming leaders; and this, of course, may induce conservative foot-dragging by the political class. Another possibility of greater interest to us is that measures of institutional reform will offer fractions of the political class glimpses of how they may survive in a more competitive political order—for instance, if previously shielded party cadres are put in the position to hold office in elected bodies; if labor fronts are freed of party controls; or if local officials are charged with local grievances. It is thus possible that glimpses and anticipations of alternative institutional roles may at long last offer those fractions that incentive to secede that, under normal circumstances, Communist regimes are least likely to offer. So an environment of choice may emerge that is closer to that which is typical of other transitions.

Whether secessions do occur; whether they have a sufficient impact to cause bandwagon effects; whether regime reformists and opposition moderates are both present in any specific case so that a convergence between them is concretely possible; whether, finally, convergence may acquire sufficient weight to offset resistance to a democratic agreement; these are questions that cannot be fully answered before we know the facts.

In the Soviet Union, at any rate, the size of the country, the size of its political class, the size and diversity of its problems (among which ethnic and nationality ones are paramount) mean that positive answers to a'l these questions are not at all certain. The difficulties may no longer lie in the special, pristine nature of the regime and the role that its political class occupied within it, nor in the presumed thinness of Soviet society and its groupings—a thinness that domestic turmoil largely belies. But the difficulties nonetheless exist. They reside in the immensity of the domestic reconversion problems with which the regime is confronted.

Unlike other dictatorships that just prefer to step down and wash their hands, the Soviet regime cannot turn away from these problems, especially because, given the size and diversity of the country's problems and the way they bring to the fore old and new societal cleavages and conflicts, a moderate opposition has not surfaced. Still, even in the Soviet Union, as we will see in the next chapter, the country's international standing, its new global responsibilities, and the very immensity of the problems it must address domestically and internationally may also work to encourage innovation by the leadership.

As to Eastern Europe (Romania excepted), one potential advantage is that steadier moderate oppositions have a greater chance to develop as a counterpart in prospective transitions. The chance is greater because Eastern Europe's societal problems are less divisive, and civil society in some of the countries has demonstrated greater capacity to refuse encroachment by an imported Communist model. The presence of a moderate opposition has a double advantage. To paraphrase a previous quote, it can, as it has in Poland with the aid of semicompetitive elections, place the regime "with its back to the wall." But, by thus creating or anticipating a stalemate (Hungary), it can also induce the regime to tolerate a more competitive system.

Last but not least, what are the trade-offs? The answer, again, is stark. One trade-off is the survival of a reformed Communist party as a significant player in a prospective multiparty system. The more the regime can anticipate the stalemate, can take the initiative in dealing with the opposition and thus preserve popular support, the more likely its survival.[27] This is perhaps the most important trade-off and the most promising it its far-ranging effects on the political class. For regimes that aspired to create new Socialist societies and assigned the single party the central role in the endeavor, and for parties born from a labor tradition of mass organization deeply rooted in twentieth-century European politics, recovering that tradition and revamping the active role of the party are not insignificant targets.[28] And because, for all the emphasis on returning to the market, Eastern European democracies that seek a place in a common European home would be reformist and interventionist in policy matters, this interventionism is another aspect that should favor the evolution of reformed communism.

I as reminded, and so, surely, are Eastern European Communist parties, of the path followed by the French and especially the Italian Communist party at the end of the war. Being unable to rule on their own and having reconciled themselves to a state of necessity, both parties became (for the first time in Communist history) important players in democratic politics. The Italian party in particular, by pursuing a more pliable strategy of adjustment to democratic politics and to changes in the Communist world, has managed to transform itself into a progressive party with, almost half a century after the war, a still significant national role.[29]

The advantage of party reforms that come from the very core of a Communist regime is that, although difficult, they carry greater legitimacy. It is one thing when radical reforms are sought by specific regime fractions and institutions that are trying, so to speak, to secede laterally; it is another when the same is done by the core leadership—that is, by the leadership of the very party to be reformed. The core cannot be held disloyal or incompetent as easily as a group of secessionists. In fact, writing about the Soviet Union, Jerry Hough argues to the contrary that the strong centralization of the Communist party gives the core relative autonomy from its political base, as well as the ability to manipulate and mobilize supporters.[30] This, plus the core's broader perspective on national interests, places it in a better position to push for policies that would transform the party. It follows that party reforms that originate from the core have a greater potential bandwagon effect on other sectors of the Communist political class. I have in mind sectors that, because of their functions, are presumably more likely to resist institutional innovations.

Left without the ideological guidance and political protection of an unreformed party, and hardly in the position to attack the leadership's new behavior openly, the less visible *nomenklaturas* (those who regulate and administer in behalf of the party; those who have a vested interest, material as much as programmatic, in the preservation of their pervasive and uncontested presence) are hardly likely to turn their foot-dragging and resistance into what I have described at various points as breakdown games.[31] After a stalemate and party reforms that foreshadow the adoption of a competitive game, it is more likely that such *nomenklaturas* would lose collective direction and resolve. This in turn, as other avenues seem to be closing, favors their recycling (and thinning out) in the service of a qualitatively different regime. Similar developments are not new in the history of European bureaucracies caught between fading dictatorship and emerging democracy.

For all intents and purposes, what we have at this point is the emergence of another trade-off, now involving the administrative classes. The trade-off at this point is not much different from that offered to Western European bureaucracies coming out of dictatorship: the reconstitution of their corporate autonomy as legally bound institutions. Such autonomy should not be unpalatable to administrative classes that—for all the overlapping of party and state and the attendant internal crypto-politics—must have come to see themselves over the years, especially in the post-totalitarian era, as performers of collective tasks. Timing, in particular, may help to make the trade-off more palatable. As typical of the way that dictatorships approach reforms in response to regime crisis, reforms of the administrative apparats will presumably have been adopted by our regimes (and in some cases they already have) before their transitions are completed. Thus, these reforms may offer the apparats those not necessarily unpleasant glimpses of how they would operate within new institutional roles that I discuss above.

Incidentally, the roles assign a new weight and value to legal accountability, thus introducing external checks and internal restraints on the pseudo-compliance with which the administrative classes (even as they are reformed) will continue to plague any new political system.

CONCLUSIONS

We are nearing the end of our journey. Because it is natural that readers tend to remember, and hold the author accountable for, what they last read, I will close the chapter, at the cost of inducing tedium by repetition, with a final reminder. My excursus on Central America and the Communist world was not meant to demonstrate that democracy is near. These are still among the trickiest places for any turn toward democracy to take place. It is no accident that I have shown greater confidence in democratic outcomes where, as in Poland, the process is already further along, and have been somewhat more guarded in assessing evolutions elsewhere. My intent, here and in the essay, has been more modest. I have not undertaken global predictions. I have pursued instead a narrower range of observations: how and why repressive regimes may have come to accept mutual tolerance over repression when trapped in a no-win prisoner's dilemma. And I have pursued prescriptions for brightening prospects, namely, what political actors can do collectively to converge toward tolerance.

But, in pursuing this line of analysis, I have aimed for something more. I have pointed out that many political actors already have those prescriptions in hand. Thus, if not near, democracy must be judged as standing a better chance. Thus, also, many set ways of understanding the prospects of democratizing stubborn dictatorships and stubborn societies may well gain from being supplemented and amended by these and similar considerations about the role of human choice.

However, to paraphrase the opening sentence of the essay, holding such a concern is not the same thing as invoking a new paradigm. Monitoring the progress of democracy needs instruments that are more sensitive to the material at hand.

CHAPTER IX

Democracy by Diffusion, Democracy by Trespassing

Democracy does not happen in an international vacuum. Because our attention has focused largely on the behavior of domestic political actors, the role of international factors deserves some final attention. International factors obviously affect domestic behavior. We have insisted throughout this essay on the importance of a domestic stalemate for propelling political actors toward a democratic agreement. But international factors may also play a similar role. One way in which they can do so is precisely by sharpening the sensation among political actors that they have indeed reached a stalemate and that the predicament is sufficiently unacceptable to warrant the search for a common understanding.

To reflect on the international dimension is to point out from yet another perspective that the prospects for democratization are not only a matter of domestic historical and systemic conditions, shared only by special countries. Hence our discussion in this chapter. To be sure, because our purpose is to illustrate how, by affecting the behavior of domestic political actors, international factors assist democratization, we will consider only those factors that have such an effect. But, obviously, this is not to say that the international dimension is always beneficial to democratization.

International factors operate in various ways. The second chapter presented two ways. The first is through the promotion of democracy exercised by foreign agents (individual states and others) on specific dictatorships or fledgling democracies. Promotion can extend from outright imposition—by, for instance, military occupation—to simple statements of support and sympathy for a successful transition. The second is through the demonstration effects that worldviews and successful examples implicitly have on specific countries and regions. But there are other ways. Without claiming to be exhaustive, we will consider two that are of special importance in contemporary transitions.

The first is the removal of a veto against democracy by a regional hegemon. One thinks immediately of Moscow and its Eastern European satellites.[1] But a similar effect may be produced when a democratic hegemon that claims overall ideological support for democracy (the United States) puts its money where its mouth is by finally abandoning its de facto and convenient tolerance of specific dependent dictatorships. The second additional way in which international factors may operate is closely connected with the one I just illustrated. It is less intuitive and more subtle, and is also tailored to fit a specific and special dictatorship, yet it is of equal importance politically and conceptually. Where the dictatorship in question is itself a hegemon (the Soviet Union) faced with a regime impasse reflecting a crisis of hegemony, its important geopolitical role demands that the impasse does not linger on. A hegemon can least afford prolonged weariness and a loss of resolve. What implications may this predicament have for regime evolutions?

Before reviewing the four ways of international influence,

and in order to understand better how they may impinge on contemporary regime changes, let us recall the basic parameters within which changes habitually occur. First, they occur at the hand of the old regime—or while the regime's political class still has some power—but also in the presence of a revived civil society. Therefore, second, convergences between regime reformers and opposition moderates become one plausible scenario for guiding changes. Hence, finally, such a scenario tends to discourage breakdown games and, in seeking a way out of a stalemate, places instead a premium on the search for toleration—a search that, I have argued, may plausibly travel all the way to a democratic agreement. How, then, are international factors promoting the scenario (and if they are not, how might they)?

DEMOCRACY BY DIFFUSION

Demonstration Effects

Demonstration effects have already received ample attention in the essay. We have used them to explain why democratic exits are more likely today. A change in worldviews toward democracy and dictatorship reflects and in turn favors a better and more realistic understanding of what democracy as an open game can offer even recalcitrant political actors, and what dictatorship cannot. Moreover, just as the record of successful authoritarian takeovers in the past may have inspired other takeovers, so also the spirit of convergence in recent democratizations may serve as an example for regime transitions that find themselves at an impasse. There is for instance little question that the experience of Spain has offered a new, previously untested, blueprint—a blueprint that some may shun, but which now nevertheless exists. Indeed, it is to that blueprint that some Communist regimes, of all regimes, have turned their attention, thus in turn serving as regional examples (or uncomfortable challenges) for their brethren.

Much more can be said about demonstration effects, but I will confine myself to recalling a comment made in the last chapter about the newly industrializing countries of Asia— for their attitude toward democracy can be a better-than-most test of the significance of those effects.[2] I commented that by their economic performance and by their relative ability to absorb labor and societal problems, these countries should feel no particular compulsion to discard their regimes. Their economic performance problems have never pushed them into a political stalemate. Therefore, if pressure for political change exists, as it does in the case of Nationalist China, and if it brings about results, as it has in the case of South Korea, demonstration effects may have to be given special credit. And the effects show up in more than one way.

These are small countries, however, with potentials and aspirations as economic and political showcases that transcend their size. Moreover, they must rely, more than others, on their success in international markets. At the same time, they are also countries that have tried to anchor the international legitimacy of their regimes on being alternatives to their Communist counterparts. The latter feature, however, has also carried with it domestic resentment, even resistance and repression, and in the case of Nationalist China a degree of international isolation. It is the combination of these international features—whereby the viability of the two regimes as showcases depends on international recognition—that may push them toward more radical political reforms. Given a supervening international context that is rediscovering the superiority of democracy and the market,[3] and given the pressure for political and economic reforms within Communist regimes, these two showcases for the economic market may become more sensitive to the convenience of restoring the political market as well.

It is not so much a question of international pressures and sanctions (which are muted at best) as it is one of the progressive obsolescence of their political formulas. Domestically and internationally, the Communist threat—even if it remained unchanged—is no longer sufficient to justify authoritarian regimes. The same can be said of justifications that rely on the political constraints of internationalized economies. The constraints do not operate in other, similarly internationalized, economies and are more difficult to sustain at home when they have become discredited abroad.

In this sense, to repeat, the two countries may offer a very revealing test of the influence exercised by demonstration effects.

Promoting Democracy

Diffuse demonstration effects often go together with a more active promotion of democracy, in words or deeds, by specific agencies. The result is pressure of some sort on nondemocratic governments, or encouragement and support for democratic forces. One good example, and a source of difference with the newly industrializing countries of Asia, where no such explicit sanction exists, is the European Economic Community's requirement that its members be democracies. The requirement played its role in the democratic transitions of southern Europe, over and above the more diffuse demonstration effects stemming from the fact that the countries of the region operated in, and interacted with, a larger democratic Europe.

Is promotion of democracy beneficial? Does it promote the kind of convergence between regime reformers and moderate opposition that, in the language of the essay, should favor democratic exits today? Or can it be ineffective and even counterproductive? The answer is mixed. The most radical form of promotion, by imposing democracy on a defeated dictatorship, is either irrelevant to contemporary democratizations or unpromising in its political effects on the host country. For one thing, the experience of Germany and Japan after the war is unlikely to repeat itself.[4] For another—given the more thorough military, political, and moral collapse of those two dictatorships—a *rapprochement* between regime and opposition was not as central to the inauguration of Japanese and especially German democracy as it would be to other inaugurations today.[5] And when room was made for reformed sectors of the old regimes during democratic reconstruction (the emperor in Japan, the military in Germany), the decision reflected international more than domestic concerns. Thus, there is little to learn from the historical examples.

Finally, the most likely way in which democracy could be imposed from the outside today would be by the direct intervention of a regional hegemon in a small country, economically and perhaps politically dependent on the hegemon (Grenada and the U.S. role in the overthrow of the Trujillo dictatorship in the Dominican Republic come to mind). However, this external intervention—despite the possibly greater discredit and weariness of the authoritarian governments being removed—has risks and costs for the relations between domestic forces caught in the intervention and its aftermath, the nature of which will become clearer after we examine more restrained forms of democratic promotion.[6]

Democratization operates today in a climate of international peace, and one in which forceful intervention for democratization is difficult and exceptional. The climate favors a fuller role for local political actors, giving international factors a role that is domestically mediated. This, however, in no way permits us to belittle more restrained forms of external democratic promotion. In the first place, external promotion is a constant, present in one way or another in practically all regime transitions. In the second place, when it is channeled through more knowledgeable and sensitive domestic actors, external promotion may be used intelligently and with significant results to turn a transition to democratic advantage. The results may not be as immediately striking as those obtained by forceful intervention. Yet, by being less rigid in its operation and less predetermined in its effects, promotion other than forceful intervention makes more room for democratic crafting. It better reveals how political actors, if offered external incentives to move toward democratization or disincentives to resist it, can respond to them by conveniently modifying their behavior.

International democratic actors can exercise various degrees of promotion in any specific case. We can for instance readily agree that if promotion is limited to expressions of generic sympathy and symbolic support, the weight of those expressions, though not irrelevant, may not be greater than that of diffuse demonstration effects, to which in fact they are akin. But we will overlook comparisons of degree. Instead, because of their policy implications, I prefer pointing to ways in which promotions that are similar in some ways (by being explicit and buttressed with deeds and material support for democratic forces) yet dissimilar in their motives and their understanding of regime and opposition may differ as to the space they leave for domestic political actors.

The contrast is fully brought out by Laurence Whitehead in a comparison of approaches to democratic promotion adopted by Western Europe and the United States.[7] Western Europe and the United States differ in motives and conduct because they differ in geopolitical roles, in democratic histories, and in internal political structures. If and when the

United States decides to promote democracy in a specific country, its policies, to paraphrase the author, are likely to be much less attentive to the relations among domestic forces in the country, much more forceful and unilateral, and much more sensitive to whether the prospective democracy will be a friend or foe. This reflects not only America's preeminent geopolitical role but also the fact that, when promotion is chosen, the role is closely embedded, in American minds, in their country's rooted democratic tradition and exclusive democratic mission.

In a Europe with a more traumatic democratic history (and a concomitant desire to heal it) but also with a lesser geopolitical role, policies toward democratizing countries tend instead to be more attentive to gradually reconstituting a community of stable democracies, whether in Europe or abroad, and less unilaterally attentive to big-power foreign-policy implications. Similarly, European policies are also more likely to be attuned to the complexities of domestic politics, even of regions as distant as Latin America, because "the political spectrum in most West European countries is reasonably congruent with that likely to emerge in Southern Europe and Latin America as they redemocratize . . . whereas the U.S. spectrum may only correspond to that ranging from the Center to the far Right, leaving emergent left-wing currents with no *interlocuteurs* in the American political process."[8]

What makes Whitehead's analysis valuable is that it is not necessary to accept its factual accuracy in order to appreciate its policy implications. The implications are that, ultimately, external agents can better help democratization if their contributions do not come at the expense of domestic political actors, particularly democratic ones, and their freedom to define their joint relations. It is one thing for foreign agents to offer incentives and disincentives, it is another to step directly into the fray. For example, if democratization seems to demand some convergence between regime and opposition, then the intervention of foreign agents (and some in particular) may well thwart that process. For one thing, they may not be able to understand how complex the process of redefining domestic relations among contending forces is. Moreover, by choosing sides, foreign agents, well-meaning though they may be, are in fact likely to increase domestic animosities.

Again, all of this strengthens the argument against the intervention of a regional or global power. When such a power makes choices among the various forces involved in shaping coalitions in the period of transition, the stigma of foreign meddling is likely to attach itself to the forces it favors. Precisely because the search for coalitions is likely to include authoritarian as well as extreme oppositional forces caught in difficult realignment maneuvers, big-power bestowal or withdrawal of democratic credentials—the more so when buttressed by selective material assistance or punishment—may disrupt or set back the maneuvers. Choosing sides and undercutting other political forces, some of which may still hold reservations about democratization, may not defeat the latter but rather cause them to curtail or reconsider their search for a modus vivendi with other forces.

This is not to say that more forceful forms of intervention are to be ruled out in all cases—including cases when a distinctly brutal regime shows itself to be impervious to rapprochement—and certainly not to say that big powers may not make a difference for the better. The simple disassociation from a crumbling oppressive regime, the revocation of support lent to domestic actors (such as the military or guerrillas) who prefer violence to rapprochement,[9] or the suspension of vetoes against certain sectors of the regime opposition may all turn out to be necessary steps toward change.

In general, a more active hegemonic intervention in situations that are still predemocratic and dominated by violence may appear more legitimate. In this sense, no other international agent is and can be more decisive than a regional hegemon in removing impediments to regional change. One may think of the United States' role in Central America to appreciate the point.

Nonetheless, a regional hegemon alone can hardly deliver change.[10] In fact, once hegemonic impediments are removed or hegemonic encouragement is offered, other international agents seem to me to be better equipped to play a role in support of domestic actors who, availing themselves of the hegemon's move, are trying to make a change. In removing the stigma of interested meddling and in facilitating the process of domestic rapprochement, there is a clear advantage if the foreign agents who wish to help and perhaps to act as formal mediators are not hegemons but agents with less at stake; that is, other countries of more equal standing in the region, or less partial supranational and regional organizations expressly created for the task or already in existence (churches, party or labor internationals, economic communities, even defense alliances).

Needless to say, in regions like Central America the mediating role of such foreign or regional agents and their ability to formulate alternatives to a long stalemate marked by ineffective violence are essential to convince violent actors of that ineffectiveness. Chapter 8 has already pointed to the role of the five regional presidents.

DEMOCRACY BY TRESPASSING

Removing Vetoes to Democracy

A hegemon that is also a dictatorship, but removes its regional veto to democracy, as the Soviet Union is now doing, does not do it because it wishes to launch a crusade for democracy. More likely, it does so only because it wishes to scuttle, under the pressure of global, regional, and domestic circumstances, its role as a hegemon. Yet there are ways in which "dehegemonization" may help regional democratization beyond the hegemon's original intentions and motives. In the previous section we discussed democracy by diffusion; here we analyze democracy by trespassing.

To be sure, the hegemon will not explicitly promote, much less force, political change in regional governments. Such actions would belie its intent to scuttle hegemony. Furthermore, although its withdrawal of the veto is critical for producing change, it could be argued that it is less than sufficient. So at least the contrasting reactions of Poland and Hungary on the one hand, the other East European nations on the other, seem to tell us. At the same time, by scuttling hegemony the Soviet Union is causing the lesser Communist regimes to lose international and domestic credibility. Their double legitimacy, or at least the fiction of their legitimacy, and the cement that held their political classes together, resided in their claimed partnership in a now obsolete global goal. Thus, the mere fact that the Soviet Union does not take sides between regimes and oppositions—its silence, its reserve, its abstention—can prove devastating. Between regimes and oppositions, it is the former, not the latter, that *need* active support and blessing. Resistance and repression could in principle substitute for legitimacy and save domestic communism. But these are not Central American dictatorships, for which endurance, at the cost of prolonging a bloody stalemate, may count more than recognition. Nor are they China, which can still claim a degree of historical legitimacy of its own and, at least comparatively, a degree of control over its political class. These are therefore regimes that the removal of fictional legitimacy and the specter of a stalemate are more likely to leave weary, without resolve, and aimless.

But necessity simplifies the choice. One plausible and previously unthinkable way out is democratization—a path on which the Soviet Union can thus set its lesser partners without expressly inviting them to take it. Whether or not the fear is well founded, it suggests the hegemon's weight that, in Poland and Hungary, both the opposition and the party reformists bent on rescuing themselves are pressing for concerted change "before it is too late"—before Mikhail Gorbachev is out of power and the hegemon changes its mind. It equally suggests the hegemon's weight that a Soviet leader—who is himself guarded when it comes to reforms in his own country and officially noncommittal when it comes to taking sides in the region—is correctly hailed (or decried) in Eastern Europe as the symbol of fundamental change.

Certainly, when it comes to regional changes, it is not difficult to understand how and why a hegemon carries more weight if it is also a dictatorship. To imagine democracy in Eastern Europe without Soviet tolerance requires a suspension of disbelief. In Central America instead, let alone South America, we have seen and can imagine countries weaving between democracy and dictatorship without American license.

But this is not the most significant difference between the two hegemons. Recent developments in the Communist world bring out a far more interesting and in fact paradoxical and unexpected side of the difference. They expose how the removal of the Soviet veto may help the democratization of Eastern Europe *more* than the U.S. promotion of democracy may help democratization in the American sphere of influence. The paradox—one of transcending, or trespassing, effects—is that the action of the Communist hegemon is not motivated by the desire to promote democracy and stays expressly clear of domestic intervention. But the paradox is lifted in part when we observe that, by comparison, the results of American promotion suffer from two types of limitations.

The first limitation has to do with the unpredictability and mixed motives of American promotion. The United States may, so to speak, overpromote democracy while also underpromoting it. In America's open and plural political system, where foreign policy need not be either bipartisan or institutionally coherent, it is not always clear and agreed upon—despite grandstanding on democracy—that the country's geopolitics, notably in its own backyard, is best served by democratic regimes. There exist disagreement and doubts as to the tenability and objectives of American regional hegemony, as well as to what types of local regimes best serve the objectives. Further, the doubts have not produced a concerted effort to reassess those objectives firmly, as the Soviet Union has recently done.[11] Therefore, even when the United States promotes democracy, its leadership is less than coherent, its implementation is haphazard and openly contested, and its results are less than decisive.

It should be clear that the purpose of our exercise is not to criticize U.S. policies but to emphasize a conceptual paradox: the paradox of Soviet trespassing effects. I take, therefore, no political solace in concluding that, on the face of it, local democratic change may be more easily set in motion by the least likely hegemon.

But there is more. The nature of dictatorships that are subject to hegemonic U.S. behavior does not help democratization in the American backyard. This is the second limitation encountered by American hegemony. Here, the contrast with the Soviet Union is less paradoxical. To recall an old point, just as the dictatorships in America's backyard can come and go, so by the same token can they endure without a shred of domestic or international legitimacy. Weariness sinks in slowly, and, short of force, American action alone can very rarely discourage and dislodge local dictatorships.

Eastern European dictatorships wish for and need instead, as best illustrated by East Germany, legitimacy and international recognition. That is why they may cling protractedly, closely, and even desperately (East Germany) to the double fiction.[12] The willingness to recognize that underneath the fiction there exists a gathering stalemate may take (has indeed taken, where the recognition has finally come) many years. And as long as the fiction is sustained by the hegemon, there is strictly speaking no stalemate as yet— no situation in which nobody wins. But once the fiction is removed by none other than the hegemon, the political and moral void that they inherit makes the other dictatorships easily and quickly prone to a political transformation that neither the hegemon nor they willed.[13]

Hegemonic Self-Reform

If Communist satellites can hardly afford prolonged weariness and a loss of resolve, then, once the global purpose that they share with the hegemon has been declared obsolete, the hegemon can afford them much less. Admittedly, it is unreasonable to argue from this that the Soviet Union is as likely as Eastern Europe to embark on radical internal political reforms more radical than it ever wished for. The previous chapter pointed to some reasons why the case for full and successful political transformation is easier to make for Eastern Europe than for the Soviet Union. Still, it also stands to reason that a hegemon faced with a domestic political impasse can least afford to prolong it.

The impasse is closely tied to Soviet efforts to reassess, indeed to scuttle, its traditional global and regional roles and to recast its international responsibilities to fit its domestic needs and the new global context. Therefore, a domestic impasse jeopardizes not only the internal governance of the Soviet Union but also, more ominously, the external standing of the Soviet Union as a great and effective power. The burden that falls on the country in view of its international status, and the need for change to succeed both domestically and internationally are in this sense uniquely compelling. To say the least, and to give the argument comparative plausibility, the compulsion to address domestic political reforms is greater for the Soviet Union than it is for a would-be hegemon like China.

In truth, if a hegemon cannot afford a domestic tug of war about the new rules of the political game, then—as usual in our scenario treatments—two scenarios for terminating the war, not just one, are imaginable. In the equation between the costs of retreating toward repression and advancing toward toleration, each scenario intervenes on a different term of the equation. In principle, we may imagine a decision to retreat to the past or to something that resembles it. Provided there is enough resolve to apply it firmly, this scenario would remove the costs of domestic toleration (the costs of abandoning post-totalitarian communism without clearly foreseeable trade-offs). But, given that the international retooling of the hegemon closely depends on the success of domestic reforms, retreating to repression, even if possible, would carry obvious external or side costs; namely, the failure of the hegemon to recast itself as a more effective and respected global partner. China may better afford this eventuality; the Soviet Union should find it unbearable.[14]

China's hegemonic role in East Asia has always been shakier—more contested by its would-be partners and would-be satellites—and at the same time less decisive for the country than the Soviet role in Eastern Europe. China's role as a global power, always defined in relation to the two super-powers, has also been less decisive for its identity. It is not inconceivable, therefore, that China's leadership may forgo an international political role it never had to reestablish do-mestic political discipline. For the country may be satisfied (and better equipped politically and economically than the Soviet Union) to combine its new authoritarianism with a position as a newly industrializing country in an internation-alized economy. If this fails, China's landmass may still withdraw behind a new continental isolationism.

CONCLUSIONS

Soviet political ambitions and global responsibilities place the Soviet Union in a different position.[15] A scenario that chooses a return to domestic repression in order to arrest a debilitating domestic impasse would deal, as stated, a dev-astating blow to the country's paramount international ob-jective—in the pursuit of which political reforms are called. Furthermore, a retreat to the past may be difficult. In order to be fully enforced, the retreat should take place before re-forms during the transition have redefined the traditional in-stitutional interests of the political class. Otherwise, if the institutional effects of reform are too advanced, then a re-treat could be doubly devastating—internationally, but also domestically. We could state this more banally: there is a powerful disincentive to attempt a retreat once there is no clear confidence that it will be fully enforced.

The Soviet Union may be reaching that point. Thus, in place of a scenario that risks taking a hegemon to the brink of international and domestic bankruptcy, a more plausible scenario is that geopolitics pushes the Soviet Union toward more transformative domestic reforms than it had bargained for. In the process, the country may learn the hard way how to shed costly and unnecessary territorial hegemony over Eastern Europe and much of its domestic empire so as to refurbish its international status.

The international responsibilities of an autocratic super-power in a global context that calls for cooperation should impress the superpower, and has impressed it, with the enormous and unbearable costs of perpetuating an ineffec-tive and discredited political order. The outcome of this sharpened awareness may not be exactly what we conven-tionally understand to be democracy, and may not, further-more, be around the corner. The essay's emphasis on the role of contingencies in regime transitions advises against social scientific venturing into long-range forecasts.

Yet, given where contingencies stand today, it is sufficient and apt to close with Friedrich Engels's words: "For what each individual wills is obstructed by everyone else, and what emerges is something that no one willed."[16] Old disagree-ments often demand new agreements.

Notes

CHAPTER I.

1. The most representative collective endeavor is Guillermo O'Donnell, Philippe Schmitter, and Laurence Whitehead, eds., *Transitions from Authoritarian Rule*, 4 vols. (Baltimore: Johns Hopkins University Press, 1986). Other literature will be cited as I proceed.

2. See, for various sources of data, G. Bingham Powell, Jr. *Contemporary Democracies* (Cambridge: Harvard University Press, 1982), pp. 2–7.

3. Samuel P. Huntington, "Will More Countries Become Democratic?" *Political Science Quarterly* 99 (Summer 1984): 218.

4. For a review of the issues on the relation between progress and democracy, see G. Bingham Powell, Jr., "Social Progress and Liberal Democracy," in *Progress and Its Discontents,* ed. Gabriel Almond et al. (Berkeley and Los Angeles: University of California Press, 1982), pp. 373–402.

5. On "politics explained by politics" and the shortcomings of sociological explanations, see Giovanni Sartori, "From the Sociology of Politics to Political Sociology," in *Politics and the Social Sciences,* ed. Seymour M. Lipset (New York: Oxford University Press, 1969), pp. 65–100.

6. Larry Diamond, Seymour M. Lipset, and Juan Linz, "Developing and Sustaining Democratic Government in the Third World" (paper delivered at the 1986 Annual Meeting of the American Political Science Association, August 28–31, Washington, D.C.). The

authors are also editors of a four-volume comparative study of democracy in the Third World. See Larry Diamond, Juan Linz, and Seymour M. Lipset, eds., *Democracy in Developing Countries* (Boulder: Lynne Rienner, 1989).

7. Myron Weiner, "Empirical Democratic Theory and the Transition from Authoritarianism to Democracy," *PS* 20 (Fall 1987): 862–63.

8. See, for example, Albert O. Hirschman, "The Search for Paradigms as a Hindrance to Understanding," *World Politics* 22 (March 1970): 329–43.

9. See the opening statement in Guillermo O'Donnell and Philippe Schmitter, *Tentative Conclusions About Uncertain Democracies,* vol. 4, of *Transitions from Authoritarian Rule,* ed. O'Donnell, Schmitter, Whitehead.

10. An excellent example of how these variables can be used is Robert A. Dahl, ed., *Political Oppositions in Western Democracies* (New Haven: Yale University Press, 1966), esp. the contributions by Dahl.

11. The statement appears in Juan Linz and Alfred Stepan, "Political Crafting of Democratic Consolidation or Destruction: European and South American Comparisons," (paper delivered at the Conference on Reinforcing Democracy in the Americas, the Carter Presidential Center, Atlanta, Georgia, November 17–18, 1986).

12. As I will clarify later on, I do not believe material policies and outcomes are a very significant part of democratic crafting.

13. If crafting is crucial, we may well ask by the same token how much room it can actually claim and how much it can accomplish. These are the kinds of questions—the most difficult in effect—that we must address. Huntington himself opens the way to one answer. He mentions a zone of transition or choice, largely coincident with the top range of middle-income countries, where authoritarian crises are likely but outcomes promise to be rather indeterminate. Presumably, it is within that zone, or similarly constructed ones, where crafting may be effective. I will pursue other conditions in the presence of which outcomes may be indetermi-

nate. I must also stress that although crafting may be more crucial and, within a range of cases, possible, this does not unfailingly mean that political elites will avail themselves of the opportunity. The reader may well ask why the opportunities for crafting may be disregarded; why, if not disregarded, they may be botched; and whether, more generally, we can identify cycles in this regard that affect the balance sheet at different historical times. For example, is there today a greater sensitivity to the delicate role of political elites in democratic transitions? This is another example of the type of question for which we are often inadequately prepared.

14. Robert A. Dahl, *Polyarchy: Participation and Opposition* (New Haven: Yale University Press, 1971).

15. Ibid., p. 208.

CHAPTER II.

1. For the distinction between descriptive and normative definitions of democracy see Jeane Kirkpatrick, "Democratic Elections, Democratic Government, and Democratic Theory," in *Democracy at the Polls: A Comparative Study of Competitive National Elections,* ed. David Butler et al. (Washington, D.C.: American Enterprise Institute, 1981), pp. 325–48.

2. See a summary of findings in G. Bingham Powell, Jr., "Social Progress and Liberal Democracy," in *Progress and Its Discontents,* ed. Gabriel Almond et al. (Berkeley and Los Angeles: University of California Press, 1982), pp. 385–89.

3. Joseph Schumpeter, *Capitalism, Socialism, and Democracy* (New York: Harper, 1942), p. 269.

4. I am taking liberties with history by leaving out the first democracy, the United States. But the United States was a cultural fragment of that corner of Europe, and similarly unique. Also, diffusion will not forcefully originate from the United States until well into the twentieth century.

5. It is of more than passing curiosity to notice that the word *democracy* was either rarely used or used in a different, more limited or negative, sense as democracy first developed. In a way, what was being developed was not clear and planned. This con-

trasts singularly with the process of diffusion, within which the word *democracy* evokes a historical experience and tangible examples.

6. I am leaving out the possibility of democracy's being "invented" anew elsewhere because (with the possible exception of the U.S. experience) it has no correspondence in reality.

7. The distinctive possibility that the birth of modern democracy partook more of the fortuitous than the nonrepeatable can be teased out of one reflection. Contemporaneous with the birth of democracy, elsewhere in Europe some of the same circumstances that accompanied its birth—i.e., the rule of law, constitutionalism, a liberal public opinion—coexisted through the nineteenth and early twentieth centuries with forms of monarchical-bureaucratic rule of absolutist derivation. Yet the rule of law, constitutionalism, and a liberal public opinion were developments without which democracy cannot even be fathomed. Why then such coexistence? One ready answer is that the birth of democracy needed more; it needed all the other circumstances listed in the text, which only a corner of Europe was blessed with. Another answer—which I prefer, without ruling out the first—is that if something as basic to human freedom as constitutionalism did not converge toward democracy elsewhere, it is because democracy was nowhere an inescapable arrangement, impersonally ordained by history. It was never a blueprint already known in its details and effects, but merely one possible artifact developed as one goes.

Nineteenth-century European rulers had two types of conflict to deal with: (1) between royal authority and public opinion, and (2) between competing strands of public opinion, as society freed itself from feudal ascription. The needed balancing answer was modern constitutionalism. What was not at all foregone is that constitutionalism would take a democratic form, one that would not just limit but expropriate rule from above. Thus it can be argued that even in the cradle of democracy, special and favorable as the local circumstances were, democracy was in the final analysis an expedient creation. It emerged in due time from a series of decisions taken by, often urged upon, political elites. These elites did not necessarily define themselves as democratic, did not work from a blueprint, and could not imagine, except when the process was well on its way, the final product. In some cases, they may have backed into some decisions. In almost all cases, their decisions were pressed upon them by the need to address concrete and immediate problems, mainly fundamental conflicts involving rulers and society.

Dankwart Rustow, writing about England, mentions among the momentous decisions the 1688 constitutional compromise, introducing limited government and closing the revolutionary conflict, and the 1832 suffrage reform, a reaction in part to the fall of the Orleanist monarchy in France. See his "Transitions to Democracy," *Comparative Politics* 2 (April 1970): 337–63. Rustow's is a pioneering essay to which we will often return.

On the rule of law and constitutionalism as European developments see Roberto Unger, *Law in Modern Society* (New York: Free Press, 1976), pp. 66–86, 134–92. On the rise of public opinion see Jürgen Habermas, *Strukturwandel der Öffentlichkeit* (Neuwied am Rhein: Hermann Luchterhand Verlag, 1962), chaps. 1–3. On the new lines of conflict emerging from the demise of the feudal order and the rise of absolutism, and on alternative constitutional responses, see Gianfranco Poggi, *The Development of the Modern State* (Stanford: Stanford University Press, 1978), chaps. 4, 5.

8. That geographical uniformity is made unnecessary by fortuitousness may escape political elites bent on replicating the successful model, or regional and global powers bent on exporting democracy. And this usually has negative consequences.

9. For these two views of democracy, which the author treats as coexisting in the formation of the American Republic, see Powell, "Social Progress," pp. 376–79.

10. An early, predemocratic example of this reversal is the lure of, before and in the first phase of the French Revolution, eighteenth-century English constitutionalism in intellectual and political circles in Paris. It seemed to some circles that England's enviably solid progress was firmly rooted in its constitutionalism. The reader may detect a hidden bias on my part for English demonstration effects. In effect, though the French and English demo-

cratic models compete within nineteenth-century Europe, the significance of the former diminishes outside Europe as time goes by. Also, save for its Jacobin/Napoleonic component, the French model pertains more to the realm of ideas than of successful practices—and ideas, though exportable, are often disappointingly difficult to implement.

11. On the role (and vagaries) of demonstration effects and reference societies in European political development, see Andrew Janos, "The Politics of Backwardness in Continental Europe, 1780–1945," *World Politics* 31 (April 1989): 325–58. See also Reinhard Bendix, *Kings or People* (Berkeley and Los Angeles: University of California Press, 1979), p. 292 and *passim*.

12. Indeed, pessimism—groundless, as it turned out—has from the very beginning surrounded the return of the defeated Axis powers to democracy following World War II.

13. The view of representative democracy as a prudential constitutional arrangement against undivided rule—by a king, an aristocrat, or a popular majority—is just as old as the Enlightenment view of democracy as the embodiment and agent of human progress. The willful optimism of the latter and its relative disregard for the ability of constitutional crafting to protect diversity contrasts with the constant constitutional concerns of, for example, the Founding Fathers. See on these points Powell, "Social Progress," pp. 376–78, and n. 1.

14. In itself, the notion that democracy may not turn out to be a universal key to progress had already occurred to some early social thinkers, who continued to see democracy as the product of progress. Bryce had already commented unfavorably on the ability of democracy to root itself in Latin American in his *South America: Observations and Impressions* (New York: Macmillan, 1911). Tocqueville, in a way, had anticipated such a line of analysis when contrasting the social bases of American democracy with the less favorable conditions in the Old World. What took longer to develop was the ability of political practitioners to anticipate the opprobrium of alternative regimes. And even more recent are the signs of a willingness to try democracy with more modest ambi-

tions. It may take witnessing that opprobrium to appreciate democracy—imperfections and all.

15. The comment applies to democratic transitions in already existing private economies. The connection between the return to political democracy and socioeconomic transformations is both closer and trickier in Communist countries because what is ambitiously at issue there is precisely the return to private market economies—a return that could expropriate Communist political classes and that also seems, however, politically necessary.

16. On these points, and especially on the return to democratic participation motivated by the desire to regain personal worth and dignity after authoritarian compliance and demobilization, see the insightful experiential account of Guillermo O'Donnell, "On the Fruitful Convergences of Hirschman's *Exit, Voice, and Loyalty* and *Shifting Involvements:* Reflections from the Recent Argentine Experience," in *Development, Democracy, and the Art of Trespassing: Essays in Honor of Albert O. Hirschman,* ed. Alejandro Foxley et al. (Notre Dame, Ind.: University of Notre Dame Press, 1986), pp. 219–68. I usually stay clear of nebulous issues such as self-worth and democracy, but O'Donnell's treatment is far from nebulous.

17. The obstacles may be domestic but also international. We should not forget that diffusion rests not only on demonstration effects but also on the direct weight of regional and global powers. I will return to this and other points about diffusion and demonstration effects in chap. 9.

18. The best English treatment of the Spanish republic in this respect is Juan Linz, "From Great Hopes to Civil War: The Breakdown of Democracy in Spain," in *The Breakdown of Democratic Regimes: Europe,* ed. Juan Linz and Alfred Stepan (Baltimore: Johns Hopkins University Press, 1978), pp. 162–215.

19. This is true at least in more recent times. Some of the postwar European forces, especially on the left, were impressed earlier on by another example—the collapse of the Weimar Republic—from which they drew a different lesson. In their eyes, Weimar collapsed because democracy gave in to increasingly reactionary

authoritarian forces and solicitations; hence the need for more advanced democracies. Spain itself was viewed in that way. Later on, the tragedy of Chile led to a reassessment of the Weimar lesson, possibly to a rediscovery of the Spanish case, and to a more balanced view of where the dangers for a new democracy might reside. The point is not the correct interpretation of historical examples, but how we often assess and reassess them in response to the historical conjunctures under which we operate.

20. One tough question is whether or how policy sacrifices are worth it (and possible) when the plural coexistence to be reestablished includes great socioeconomic inequalities, deep enough to raise troubling issues of social injustice. Should coexistence be reestablished, prior and decisive as the task is in the short run, without somehow addressing the issue of injustice? The question is addressed in chaps. 5 and 6.

21. Reliance, even in political science, on sociological functionalism, in the tradition of Durkheim and Spencer rather than Tocqueville, explains in part the extraordinary ability of the paradigms to disregard the historical fact that paths to development, social and political, did not converge (not yet?).

22. Andrew Janos, *Politics and Paradigms: Changing Theories of Change in Social Science* (Stanford: Stanford University Press, 1986), chaps. 2, 3. Janos offers a very extensive analysis of the relevant literature, along the lines I follow in the text.

23. The founder of this literature is Seymour M. Lipset, *Political Man* (Garden City, N.Y.: Doubleday, 1960). A critical review of the ample literature is John D. May, *Of the Conditions and Measures of Democracy* (Morristown, N.J.: General Learning Press, 1973). The logic of Robert Dahl's *Polyarchy*, which we took as a foil in the introductory chapter, is akin to this literature. One well-known criticism of the literature, which is not decisive for our counternarrative, is its tendency to confuse genetic and maintenance theories of democracy, mainly by using evidence from the latter as if it were evidence of why democracies come about.

24. The contrast may provide an intellectual clue to why fears of democratic instability and authoritarian involutions in postwar Europe went together with the elaboration of nondemocratic mo-

bilization models for the Third World. What was culturally acceptable and therefore theorized for the Third World—the costs of mobilization for the community—was not acceptable for more advanced Europe.

25. There are a few scholars who have paid attention to this issue all along. Some I have mentioned; some will appear later on.

CHAPTER III.

1. Robert A. Dahl, *Polyarchy: Participation and Opposition* (New Haven: Yale University Press, 1971), p. 16.

2. As we know from chap. 1, there is more to Dahl's analysis than objective circumstances. In his postscript to *Polyarchy,* he also examines how the lack of objective circumstances that favor mutual security can be remedied by actors purposely seeking mutual guarantees. In the light of this, his famous opening axiom (p. 15) concerning the greater likelihood that a competitive regime will develop if the costs of suppression exceed those of toleration, can be read to say that such a regime is more likely if, during the transition to it, the costs of tolerating opposition are *made* to be lower than those of suppression—if, in other words, the costs for a nondemocratic government of switching to a competitive regime are made lower than those of remaining nondemocratic. And this in fact falls within the perspective that I am about to discuss in the text.

3. It follows that I am not advocating replacing Dahl's hypothesis about coexistence (the higher the level of conflict, the less likely the establishment of coexistence in diversity) with its opposite. At such a level of blunt generality, both hypotheses lose cogency.

4. Dankwart Rustow, "Transitions to Democracy," *Comparative Politics* 2 (April 1970): 362.

5. The accent on forestalling conflict is worth noticing because it places attention on the role of perceptions and anticipations. There may be no clear long-standing authoritarian crisis yet, but one may be anticipated. In such a case, choosing democracy reflects a calculated bet that conflict within a legitimate democratic frame is preferable. Such a strategy is actually very much in keeping with Dahl's famous axiom. The Spanish transition comes read-

ily to mind as the classic case. Another, more concerted effort to forestall conflict was the package of institutional guarantees adopted by Sweden between 1902 and 1907. Sweden is discussed by Rustow himself in his *Politics of Compromise: A Study of Parties and Cabinet Government in Sweden* (Princeton: Princeton University Press, 1955), chaps. 1–3.

6. Rustow, "Transitions to Democracy," p. 362.

7. As a small child, but somehow already an anti-Fascist, I was taken aback by my father's comment at the fall of fascism ("Yesterday everybody was a fascist; today everybody is a democrat"). Yet, for all its cynicism, the statement was not far from the truth. But was the cynicism warranted? The psychology of most conversions—accompanied as they are by behaviors that range from indifference toward the old regime, yet tinged perhaps with nostalgia, to heretical zeal against it—is too complex to be reduced to cynical calculations and self-serving deceptions. One may also notice, to counter cynicism, the long-standing and widespread popular rejection of communism in Communist countries.

8. For example, even taking for granted that a cultural tradition attuned to democracy existed in the first transitions to democracy (the classic English case), I am suggesting that in the more rapid and contentious transitions of recent times the missing benefit has been, and could be replaced successfully by, individual conversions coinciding with the personal trauma brought by authoritarianism and its crisis. As implied in n. 7, most citizens faced with a regime crisis are forced to come to terms with a past that they have passively or ambiguously witnessed. Their conversion, therefore, is a response to more complex—possibly defensive or cathartic—psychic needs. And though the conversions may not reflect the type of rational elite calculations that we are discussing in the text, they can become quite an asset in eventually directing the regime crisis toward a calculated democratic exit.

9. Adam Przeworski, "Some Problems in the Study of the Transition to Democracy," in *Transitions from Authoritarian Rule: Comparative Perspectives,* ed. Guillermo O'Donnell, Philippe Schmitter, and Laurence Whitehead (Baltimore: Johns Hopkins University Press, 1986), pp. 47–63.

10. Ibid.

11. There is a contrast, here, with transitions from democracy to authoritarianism. Authoritarianism does not have to define itself for the benefit of prospective supporters but may succeed with a negative platform (e.g., stopping democratic anarchy; *"on s'engage et puis on voit"*).

12. In the article cited in n. 9, Przeworski argues outright that the concept of legitimacy (and, implicitly, its derivatives: legitimation, loyalty, allegiance, trust, consensus, David Easton's "diffuse support") are unnecessary in that the mental readiness implied by these terms can be reduced invariably to a calculus of interests. See also Adam Przeworski, "Material Bases of Consent: Economics and Politics in a Hegemonic System," in *Political Power and Social Theory,* vol. 1, ed. Maurice Zeitlin (Greenwich, Conn.: JAI Press, 1980), esp. pp. 33–34.

13. Dahl, *Polyarchy,* pp. 40–47; Samuel P. Huntington, "Will More Countries Become Democratic?" *Political Science Quarterly* 99 (Summer 1984): 209–14; Alfred Stepan, "Paths Toward Redemocratization: Theoretical and Comparative Considerations," in *Transitions from Authoritarian Rule: Comparative Perspectives,* ed. O'Donnell et al., pp. 64–84; Enrique A. Baloyra, ed., *Comparing New Democracies* (Boulder: Westview, 1987), pp. 9–52; and Leonardo Morlino, "Democratic Establishments," in ibid., pp. 53–78.

14. Another special factor that favored the removal of the legacy in the four countries is the presence, to which I shall return, of democracy or constitutionalism in their past.

15. I am following in this section my argument in "Government Performance: An Issue and Three Cases in Search of Theory," *West European Politics* 7 (April 1984): 172–87.

16. See, with reference to Latin America, Guillermo O'Donnell, "The United States, Latin America, Democracy: Variations on a Very Old Theme," in *The United States and Latin America in the 1980s,* ed. Kevin J. Middlebrook and Carlos Rico (Pittsburgh: University of Pittsburgh Press, 1986), pp. 353–77.

17. See on these points Baloyra, *Comparing New Democracies,* esp. pp. 36–42. Generational discontinuity has been typical

of the more traditional or the older dictatorships: the holdovers from interwar fascism, which (like Portugal and Spain) have lost their original purpose along the way, or long-standing Communist regimes. Institutional conflict seems more central to Latin America's bureaucratic-authoritarian regimes, where the military as an institution is pivot (and prisoner) of the regimes' national development and security ideology. See on the latter, Alfred Stepan, *Rethinking Military Politics* (Princeton: Princeton University Press, 1988).

18. Hirschman discusses unintended consequences of human action and their relation to change—with particular regard to how action to conserve can lead to innovation—in his *Bias for Hope* (New Haven: Yale University Press, 1971), pp. 31–37. It seems that the French saying *plus ça change, plus c'est la même chose,* more than reflecting common wisdom reflects instead the state of mind of those who—by function, status, aspirations, profession, or whatever—wish to believe in it.

19. Two classic statements on the distinction between authoritarianism and totalitarianism are by Juan Linz: "An Authoritarian Regime: The Case of Spain," in *Cleavages, Ideologies and Party Systems,* ed. Erik Allard and Yrjo Littunen (Helsinki: Westermarck Society, 1964), pp. 291–341; "Totalitarian and Authoritarian Regimes," in *Handbook of Political Science,* ed. Fred I. Greenstein and Nelson W. Polsby (Reading, Mass.: Addison-Wesley, 1975), vol. 3, *Macropolitical Theory,* pp. 175–411. The latter essay also discusses post-totalitarian regimes as a special category of authoritarianism.

20. In addition, the overthrow is not likely to bring about democracy, but some form of disguised "popular" dictatorship or guided democracy. The point will become clearer in the next chapter.

21. What response is chosen may depend—in addition to the consistency, cohesiveness, ideological makeup, and strategic preferences of the opposition—on the regime's perception of itself, its own resources, its own internal cohesiveness and extended reach. See Baloyra, *Comparing New Democracies,* pp. 40–42.

22. Indeed, notice how, with the crisis of communism, left and

right have lost their historical connotations. Under Communist regimes, a "leftist" is almost anybody who does not compromise and wants radical measures against the Communist legacy of government. A rightist is a member of the regime—with the hard core constituting the extreme right wing.

23. Guillermo O'Donnell, who pays special attention to the strategic interaction between actors with different strategic attitudes toward the transition, also makes special room in his analysis for neutral and uncommitted actors. Mobilizing them in the right direction may be seen in some ways as the ultimate strategic move. See more recently, O'Donnell, "Notes for the Study of Democratic Consolidation in Latin America" (unpublished paper, Kellogg Institute, University of Notre Dame, December 1985).

24. A much jauntier view, limited to Latin America, of these and related matters is taken by Daniel Levine in his review of the work edited by O'Donnell, Schmitter, and Whitehead. Levine argues that greater importance should be accorded to the actual extent and weight of democratic commitment, and less to the view of democracy as a second-best choice as well as to the weight of nondemocratic players. Daniel Levine, "Paradigm Lost: Dependence to Democracy," *World Politics* 40 (April 1988): 377–94.

25. One exception is represented by consociational democracies, which employ preordained noncompetitive formulas in the allocation especially of politico-institutional positions. Noncompetitive formulas to accommodate various social and institutional constituencies are more likely to be found in dictatorships—especially authoritarian—that may use them in forging their coalitions. Because these formulas become stereotyped over time and often no prescribed rules exist to alter them, infighting and discontinuities with no clear exit may ensue.

26. Przeworski, *operibus citatis*.

27. I am following here my "Party Government and Democratic Reproducibility: The Dilemma of New Democracies," in *Visions and Realities of Party Government,* ed. Francis G. Castles and Rudolf Wildenmann (Berlin: de Gruyter, 1986), pp. 178–204.

28. Robert A. Dahl, *After the Revolution?* (New Haven: Yale University Press, 1970), p. 12.

CHAPTER IV.

1. Nearly as important as adopting democratic rules is knowing how to adopt them: how to time them with respect to each other; what priority they should receive with respect to other processes, tasks, and reconstruction policies; how to employ them as leverage for alliances and coalitions; and what institutional and informal settings, what styles of interaction, to employ in processing them. The point is that, just as the rules make a difference, so does the way in which they are adopted. This is part of next chapter's topic.

2. This is very close to Dahl's formulation of the role of mutual guarantees in his postscript:

> Opponents in a conflict cannot be expected to tolerate one another if one of them believes that toleration of another will lead to his own destruction or severe suffering. Toleration is more likely to be extended and to endure only among groups which are not expected to damage one another severely. Thus the costs of toleration can be lowered by effective mutual guarantees against destruction, extreme coercion, or severe damage. Hence a strategy of liberalization requires a search for such guarantees. (*Polyarchy: Participation and Opposition* [New Haven: Yale University Press, 1971], pp. 217–18.)

3. Giuseppe Di Palma, "Party Government and Democratic Reproducibility: A Dilemma of New Democracies," in *Visions and Realities of Party Government,* ed. Francis G. Castles and Rudolf Wildenmann (Berlin and New York: de Gruyter, 1986). I am using the Italian words because Italy is probably the best example of *garantismo*'s application.

4. The advantages of this early path are discussed in Robert A. Dahl, *Polyarchy,* chap. 1.

5. There are two points of difference between the German and the Japanese transitions. On the one hand, the American commitment to the reconstruction of Japan along democratic lines shows a "Jacobin" drive not found in Germany. On the other hand, and

more important, Japan's old regime came to play an apparently subservient yet significant role in the reconstruction that has no parallels in Germany. On Japan see Arthur E. Tiedemann, "Japan Sheds Dictatorship," in *From Dictatorship to Democracy,* ed. John H. Herz (Westport, Conn.: Greenwood Press, 1982). As for the Italian transition from defeated fascism to democracy, it too had to come to terms with reluctant players in ways that I will discuss later in the chapter.

6. It should be clear, therefore, that I propose a less than comprehensive theory of crafting, offering a highly specific typology of crafting choices, their causes and consequences. Mine is more modestly an interpretive exercise that seeks to understand what securing a new democracy consists in. That is why I propose instead a few illustrative scenarios. Abstracted in part from the experience of instructive cases, these scenarios seem more appropriate for that exercise. Besides, I fear that a more comprehensive theory would convey the false impression that paths to democratization are finite. I prefer the risk of being incomplete.

7. In point of fact, improbable though the scenarios (at least the first two) and their positive outcomes may appear to some readers, the open question is whether they will stay improbable given the record of transitions. And the ultimate answer should be that—because learning, personal awareness, changing opinion climates, and other subjective factors come into play as time frames change—we cannot extrapolate from the present. We can, instead, speculate against it.

8. This and the other scenarios are reelaborations of scenarios presented in Di Palma, "Party Government and Democratic Reproducibility," sec. 2.

9. This was the position of the Marxist left in Italy's transition from fascism.

10. Guillermo O'Donnell and Philippe Schmitter consider a *democradura* a typical phase in the transition to democracy. I am interested in finding a shortcut in this phase. See O'Donnell and Schmitter, *Transitions from Authoritarian Rule: Tentative Conclusions about Uncertain Democracies* (Baltimore: Johns Hopkins University Press, 1986), pp. 40–45.

11. I will discuss in chap. 5 why postponements in the process of democratization can be a recipe for failure.

12. There are points of similarity between *garantismo* and the practice of consociationalism—at least in their intent to protect minorities, to seek mutual guarantees, to deny the prediction that people cannot coexist in diversity. However, consociationalism is in effect a noncompetitive answer—in some ways the opposite of *garantismo*'s randomness and uncertainty. In the previous chapter I suggest why in our scenario consociationalism may not be acceptable, save as an emergency measure limited to the transition, to any but the most reluctant sectors of the seceding right. In the medium run, it can create a stalemated political environment particularly deleterious to the civilian forces that are co-opted in it. Shielded and isolated from accountability and competition, they may lose touch with society. And because their political appeals or social composition may change, difficult renegotiations of the consociational terms may be needed. In sum, consociationalism may become a throwback to *democradura*. In a paper entitled "On Consociationalism in the Brazilian Context" (presented at the Conference on Constitutionalism and Democracy: Political Institutions for the Twenty-first Century, Brasilia, May 1987), I discuss at greater length this and other limits of consociationalism. They include the danger of arresting the rise of a socially rooted representative party system in countries where the problem for democracy is, not socially rooted partisan conflict, but weak parties poorly implanted in a context of social disaggregation and fragmentation. By comparison, *garantismo* may not treat, but neither does it aggravate, the inability of a society to represent itself politically.

13. Juan Linz has written repeatedly about presidentialism versus parliamentarism as a choice in contemporary transitions to democracy. I can do no better than paraphrase his argument. The winner-take-all logic of presidentialism; the fixity of the presidential terms of office; the fact that presidential government is not made of parliamentarians, does not need parliamentary support, but also cannot rely on it; and much more—all contribute to mak-

ing presidentialism a rigid and awkward, rather than a strong, instrument for reconciliation in a new democracy. As an instrument for representation it forces a polarization of electoral competition and leaves losing candidates with no office. By contrast, in a parliamentary system there are no pressures for polarizing alliances to win the presidency. At the same time, appropriate electoral laws can safeguard the parliamentary representation of winners and losers alike and still avoid an excessive fragmentation of the party system. As an instrument of government, parliamentarism offers its governing elites coalitional flexibility, as well as the opportunity to endure, to resume action in parliament when out of office. Presidentialism has no such flexibility.

Nor is the notion that presidentialism introduces a beneficial system of checks and balances correct. A president can rarely perform the moderating role that a head of state performs in a parliamentary system. In the last analysis, he is an elected partisan. As to the presence, separate from the president, of an equally elected parliament, chances are that (unless president and parliament are expressions of the same majority) it will produce an often unreconcilable duality of powers, each appealing to its own source of legitimacy. Only in the United States, for reasons that go beyond the constitutional intent of presidentialism and have to do with the American party system and other American constitutional features, has presidentialism operated as a system of countervailing powers. See Juan Linz, "Democracy: Presidential or Parliamentary. Does it Make a Difference?" (presented at the Workshop on Political Parties in the Southern Cone, sponsored by the World Peace Foundation and the Woodrow Wilson International Center for Scholars, Smithsonian Institution, Washington, D.C., July 1985).

Linz's remarks do not bode well for Latin America, where presidentialism has a long tradition. Repeatedly, in countries like Argentina (similarly in the Philippines after Marcos) presidentialism has contributed to the difficulties of democratization. More recently, we have seen attempts in Poland to use some features of presidentialism unconventionally, as part of a larger scheme to share power, by giving the presidency to the regime while opening parliament and government to the opposition. Notice, however, that this is an arrangement pursued within a predemocratic consociational context to forestall or slow down full democratization.

14. Powell provides evidence that *garantismo* cuts the cost of toleration. Comparing systematic evidence on presidential, majoritarian, and representational systems, Powell comments that the last system (a close version of *garantismo*) has never used government powers to overthrow or suspend democratic processes. He writes: "The representational systems did, for the most part, work as their design suggests: bringing most groups into the political arena, giving them some policy making role, and emphasizing the linkages between all citizens and the democratic processes of government" (p. 224). Because his evidence also shows that in almost no representational system did democracy collapse because of civil war (exception: Lebanon) or electoral victory by the extremes (exception: Weimar), *garantismo* has so far worked better than presidentialism and majoritarian systems to keep democracy going. One cautionary note from Powell's evidence: "The representational parliamentary systems can be quite vulnerable to military intervention *if the major parties cannot act together* to support the system" (p. 225; emphasis added). See G. Bingham Powell, Jr., *Contemporary Democracies: Participation, Stability, and Violence* (Cambridge: Harvard University Press, 1982), pp. 224–25; p. 171, table 8-2.

15. Again, Powell reports evidence that representational systems help the entry of potentially disaffected groups in the democratic game. The groups turn their activity to legitimate political channels and away from protest—thus helping democratic stability. See Powell, ibid., pp. 206, 222–23.

16. The notion that institutions that have served an authoritarian regime (an army in particular) maintain a primary interest in running or supervising politics is often misplaced. On this point, with reference to the military, Juan Linz has written extensively and eloquently. See for example his "Totalitarian and Authoritarian Regimes," in *Handbook of Political Science*, vol. 3, ed. Fred I. Greenstein and Nelson W. Polsby (Reading, Mass.: Addison-Wesley, 1975). Another important contribution focused on the role of

the military in the transitions is Alfred Stepan, *Rethinking Military Politics* (Princeton: Princeton University Press, 1988).

17. Conversely, if democratic actors do not move to seize the occasion, festering suspicion and circumspection may prevail. I have already hinted at the need for democratic options to emerge quickly.

18. On the importance of this bandwagon effect for macrosocial change, see Thomas C. Schelling, *Micromotives and Macrobehavior* (New York: Norton, 1978), chap. 7.

19. For further details on democratic reconstruction and the onset of *garantismo,* see my "Italy: Is There a Legacy and Is It Fascist?" in *From Dictatorship to Democracy,* ed. John H. Herz. See also Leonardo Morlino, "Del fascismo a una democracia débil. El cambio de régimen en Italia (1939–1948)," in *Transición a la democracia en el sur de Europa y América Latina,* ed. Julian Santamaria (Madrid: Centro de Investigaciones Sociológicas, 1981).

20. Interview conducted by Donald Share in January 1982 and reported in his "Two Transitions: Democratization and the Evolution of the Spanish Socialist Left," *West European Politics* 8 (January 1985): 92.

21. Giuseppe Di Palma, "Founding Coalitions in Southern Europe: Legitimacy and Hegemony," *Government and Opposition* 15 (Spring 1980): 162.

22. Such a change of practices is much more difficult in the first scenario. This does not make a democracy that emerges from that scenario necessarily weaker, but we will see that it makes the mechanisms of performance and survival different.

23. I have been cautioned by some colleagues that deriving scenarios from reality only to reapply them to reality, is a methodological abomination: nothing is explained. But whether scenarios are first inspired by actual occurrences or by a set of axioms is not of great relevance. The real point is what scenarios, however derived, are good for. Assuredly, they are never tools for systematic prediction of all occurrences. They are, as already stated (n. 6), tools for interpreting/explaining limited and bounded ranges of occurrences. That is why I assign great importance to their *internal* plausibility. There is, therefore, no reason for disappointment. Even if they are of concrete derivation, this does not demote sce-

narios to a theoretically barren restatement of actual occurrences. They are still designed, and can still be employed, to transform concrete and apparently linear events into contingencies. Thus, scenarios are models or abstractions—not narrative, or theory, but a guide, and one that needs retranslation when applied again to reality. See on this point, A. Feit, "Insurgency in Organizations: A Theoretical Analysis," *General Systems* 14 (1969): 157.

Max Gluckman (in *Politics, Law and Ritual in Tribal Society* [Oxford: Oxford University Press, 1965], p. 286) writes that each radical change results from a unique complex of many events that can be understood only through narrative. Scenarios are a guide through that narrative. Thus, one could adapt our "Spanish" scenario to make sense of transitions in other cases where democratization is taken up by the old regime—for example, South Korea. One interesting development in South Korea's transition was the reaction of newly elected president Roh Tae Woo to the unexpected defeat of the presidential party in the parliamentary elections of spring 1988. Despite presidentialism and its prerogatives—which, we have seen, raise potential obstacles to democratization—the new president chose to bolster the role of parliament by seeking greater cooperation with the opposition parties and by removing hard-liners from his government. This recalls the comment in the text, promoted by the Spanish case, that reformers coming from the old regime need the support of the forces to their left, and that such support carries political sacrifices. That need is clearer when those forces gather strength and electoral legitimacy.

24. The major point on which Spain departs from the scenario is that, the transition over, the party that controlled it suffered a devastating setback. Not only was the Democratic Center Union (UCD) replaced in government by the Socialists; it has practically disappeared from the electoral map (without another moderate party fully replacing it). According to Richard Gunther's persuasive interpretation, the success of the party in mastering the transition explains its demise. Not geared for normal party politics, but rather to making democracy a success, the party exhausted itself on the latter task. See his "El Hundimiento de UCD," in *Crisis y Cam-*

bio: Electores y Partidos en la España de los Años Ochenta, ed. Juan Linz and José Montero (Madrid: Centro de Estudios Constitucionales, 1986). See also Richard Gunther, Giacomo Sani, and Goldie Shabad, eds., *Spain after Franco: The Making of a Competitive Party System* (Berkeley and Los Angeles: University of California Press, 1988).

25. The literature on the Spanish transition—both articles and books—is overabundant. In addition to the books just cited, which offer a thoroughly researched and documented retrospective, see also Donald Share, *The Making of Spanish Democracy* (New York: Praeger, 1986), which offers an analysis close in many ways to mine.

26. A populist left can denounce the limits of mere electioneering, but it may not be able/willing to ban elections; for most people elections are still an essential and coveted expression of mass politics.

27. Portugal not being as much a success story as Spain must be one reason why the literature on the Portuguese transition is not as abundant. Two useful collections are Lawrence S. Graham and Douglas Wheeler, eds., *In Search of Modern Portugal: The Revolution and Its Consequences* (Madison: University of Wisconsin Press, 1983); Lawrence S. Graham and Harry M. Makler, eds., *Contemporary Portugal: The Revolution and Its Antecedents* (Austin: University of Texas Press, 1979).

CHAPTER V.

1. Juan Linz, "Il fattore tempo nei mutamenti di regime," *Teoria Politica* 2, no. 1 (1986): 16–18.

2. On elections in postauthoritarian regimes see a number of contributions in Myron Weiner and Ergun Ozbudun, eds., *Competitive Elections in Developing Countries* (Durham, N.C.: Duke University Press, 1987).

3. I am leaving aside for the moment the question of what it takes *concretely* to convince secessionists to abandon their natural inclination for caution and to transact a speedier democratization. Understanding the costs of caution may not be sufficient.

4. I am stressing early elections as an important signal, but

secessionist governments can give other signals of their good faith. A clear one is the willingness of the government to embark on a constitution-making process, co-opting on the way other political forces. As we saw in last chapter's "Spanish" scenario of a transition directed from above, such a transition not only recommends that *garantista* rules be adopted but also recommends that, in keeping with their spirit, the rules be crafted in cooperation.

5. Larry Diamond makes a stronger case for the capacity of liberalization to alleviate skepticism and for the virtues of gradual transitions. See his "Beyond Authoritarianism and Totaliarianism: Strategies for Democratization," *Washington Quarterly*, 12 (Winter 1989): 141–63.

6. The equally supervised but faster and more clearly committed Spanish transition has avoided those pitfalls. See the contrast in Donald Share and Scott Mainwaring, "Transition from Above: Democratization in Brazil and Spain," in *Political Liberalization in Brazil*, ed. Wayne A. Selcher (Boulder: Westview, 1988). Terry Karl refers specifically to Brazil in her argument that pacts and "impositions" (transitions unilaterally guided from above) are the only available options in Latin America. Here assessment in convincing. But the costs of slowness, not a necessary ingredient of imposition, remain. See Terry Karl, "Dilemmas of Democratization in Latin America" (paper presented at the Conference on Latin America at the Threshold of the 1990s, Beijing, June 8–16, 1988).

7. On elections in El Salvador see Terry Karl, "Imposing Consent: Elections versus Democratization in El Salvador," in *Elections in Latin America in the 1980s,* ed. Paul Drake and Eduardo Silva (San Diego: Center for U.S.-Mexican Studies, University of California, San Diego, 1985).

8. In his paper on transitions ("Transitions to Democracy," *Comparative Politics* 2 [April, 1970]: 337–63), Dankwart Rustow argues both sides of the argument. He argues that transitions are not completed and democracy is not safe without a final phase of habituation lasting at least one generation. As he puts it, a democracy's "conspicuous failure to resolve some urgent political question . . . early in the habituation phase . . . may prove fatal" (p. 359). But he also argues that habituation only follows a decisional

phase in which formal democratic rules are clearly instituted and made operational. It is the concrete operation of these rules that makes habituation possible, indeed likely—not vice versa.

9. The borderline is not always clear. Street demonstrations may be meant, not to rock democratization, but to influence it. Yet they may produce the former effect by raising the risk of conservative backlashes. The ultimate criterion is not behavioral motivations but effects—whether or not intended. Naturally, to complicate matters, political actors concerned with disruption must often anticipate whether certain behaviors will be disruptive, and will use the opportunity to prejudge the case.

10. O'Donnell and Schmitter discuss sequences, but their notion of a military pact is different from mine. See Guillermo O'Donnell and Philippe Schmitter, *Transitions from Authoritarian Rule: Tentative Conclusions about Uncertain Democracies* (Baltimore: Johns Hopkins University Press, 1986), chap. 4.

11. The assumption is too broad to be more than indicative. I let it stand for purposes of economy. Neither the bourgeoisie nor the political right is a homogeneous category. Nor, in a transition context of shifting alliances, are the significance and consequences of such identification that firm and predictable.

12. The problems of accommodating business, responding to labor demands, and dealing with economic downturns in a capitalist context are salient in southern European and especially Latin American transitions. They are less salient in the newly industrializing countries of Asia. On Latin America, see John Sheahan, "Economic Policies and the Prospects for Successful Transition from Authoritarian Rule in Latin America," in *Transitions from Authoritarian Rule: Comparative Perspectives*, ed. O'Donnell, Schmitter, and Whitehead (Baltimore: Johns Hopkins University Press, 1986); and Barbara Stallings and Robert Kaufman, eds., *Debt and Democracy in Latin America* (Boulder: Westview, 1989).

13. Again, the contrast between the Spanish and the Brazilian transition is instructive. In Spain, economic pacts (the *Pactos de la Moncloa*) were struck at the beginning of the constitution-making period. In Brazil, protracted wrangling over constitutional issues induced the political parties to stall action on the debt issue until

after the approval of the constitution. On the point, see, for Brazil, in addition to the references above, Eul-Soo Pang, "Debt, Adjustment, and Democratic Cacophony in Brazil," in *Debt and Democracy,* ed. Stallings and Kaufman.

14. Franklin Adler argues that one reason fascism appealed more strongly to Italian landowners than to industrialists was that the former lacked cohesive business associations for dealing more effectively with labor pressures and economic downturns in a democratic context. See Franklin H. Adler, "Italian Industrialists from Liberalism to Fascism" (Ph.D. diss., University of Chicago, 1980).

15. One of the best historical illustrations of a constitutional tradition cast in an autocratic mold is the nineteenth-century German *rechtsstaat.* Public law under the *rechtsstaat* claimed a distinctive socioscientific role in the search for and definition of the collective welfare. Other constitutional traditions, though anchored to the same legal-rational core, followed more liberal paths. On the contrast between constitutional traditions, see Guido De Ruggiero, *The History of European Liberalism* (Gloucester, Mass.: Peter Smith, 1981).

16. The coincidence of interests, however, holds much less when transitions occur in countries where the state has no history of autonomy and impersonality, but one instead of primitive parasitism. Thus, for instance, in the dynastic or military patrimonial regimes of the Middle East and Central America, where public functions are privatized and the state operates intermittently, the offer of legal-rational guarantees under democracy holds limited appeal for the state apparatus. What avenues are open to democracy in such regimes is a matter for analysis in the last chapter.

17. Research on contemporary Latin America, and Brazil in particular, offers good evidence that business often had only ad hoc, sporadic, and individualized access to authoritarian governments and their policy processes, that this negatively affected its associationism, and that business has therefore played a role in the growing public resentment against those governments. These points are treated for Brazil in Ben Ross Schneider, "Framing the State: Economic Policy and Political Representation in Post-Authoritarian Brazil," in *State and Society in Brazil: Continuities and*

Changes, ed. John Wirth et al. (Boulder: Westview, 1987); and Fernando Enrique Cardoso, *Autoritarismo e Democratização* (Rio de Janeiro: Paz e Terra, 1975), and "Entrepreneurs and the Transition Process: The Brazilian Case," in *Transitions from Authoritarian Rule: Latin America,* ed. O'Donnell, Schmitter, Whitehead. For a general view of business in the democratic transitions of Latin America, see Sylvia Maxfield, "National Business, Debt-Led Growth and Political Transition in Latin America," in *Debt and Democracy,* ed. Stallings and Kaufman.

18. See on these points Adam Przeworski, "Material Bases of Consent: Economics and Politics in a Hegemonic System," in *Political Power and Social Theory,* ed. Maurice Zeitlin (Greenwich, Conn.: JAI Press, 1980), vol. 1, pp. 25–28.

19. The term *social contract* in Eastern European literature refers to an implicit system of reciprocity between regimes and civil society, which developed after Khrushchev and in which the regimes obtain political support in exchange for a set of trimmed down but predictable social and material benefits. The term *welfare-state authoritarianism* has also been employed. See George Breslauer, "On the Adaptability of Soviet Welfare State Authoritarianism," in *Soviet Society and the Communist Party,* ed. Karl W. Riavec (Amherst: University of Massachusetts Press, 1978); and Walter D. Conner, "Workers, Politics, and Class Consciousness," in *Industrial Labor in the U.S.S.R.,* ed. Arcadius Kahan and Blair Ruble, (New York: Pergamon, 1979).

20. We may, on the other hand, take comfort in the possibility that trade-off tactics are not that urgent in other scenarios; for example, in the newly industrializing countries of Asia. There, models of economic growth, prevailing industrial and state-interest relations, the early dismantling of traditional agrarian relations, as well as the changing social composition of labor may ease the self-adaptation of corporate interests—whether of the state, business, or labor—to a nascent democracy. It follows that the conservative mood that accompanies most contemporary transitions should have, in these cases, limited social and political costs. In a way, the factors that account for the economic success of the newly industrializing countries are the same ones that ease class

adjustment to democracy. On the other hand, the very fact that their regimes are not experiencing a crisis of material performance may mean that, on this aspect, there is no sufficient cause for political crisis. Interesting material on economic and class relations, and the intervening role of economic compromises, in the choice between democracy and authoritarianism is found in Hyug Baeg Im, "The Rise of Bureaucratic Authoritarianism in South Korea," *World Politics* 39 (January 1987): 231–57.

21. It should be clear from the thrust of my argument that the trade-offs would differ from the politically more cramped consociational practices discussed in the previous chapter. Though encompassing the negotiation of joint sacrifices, the trade-offs still include the creation of an openly competitive political system hinging on the recognition, indeed the fostering, of a popular opposition.

22. See on this point O'Donnell and Schmitter, *Transitions from Authoritarian Rule: Tentative Conclusions,* pp. 46–47. It is worth remembering that divisions internal to labor and business may hurt, but they also help by fostering defections by intransigents. They may also create bandwagon effects around sectors of labor and business that, feeling unencumbered by a unity yet to come, are readier to risk accommodations.

23. In addition to the essay by Sylvia Maxfield in *Debt and Democracy,* ed. Stallings and Kaufman, see in the same volume Ian Roxborough, "Labor: A Major Victim of the Debt Crisis."

24. In the article cited above, Larry Diamond, referring to the conditions for democratization "in countries like Mexico, or to a more extreme degree, the Soviet Union," writes that "the situation may be more delicate and intractable . . . where the hegemonic party has spun a vast network of patrons, bosses and bureaucrats whose statuses, careers and livelihoods . . . would be threatened by democratization" (p. 147).

25. For the way in which Eastern European regimes would prefer to understand the concept of democratic pluralism, see James P. Scanlan, "Reforms and Civil Society in the USSR," *Problems of Communism* 37 (March–April 1988): 41–46.

26. The case is argued eloquently and at length by Guillermo O'Donnell, who considers dealing with the social injustice and au-

thoritarian relations that permeate Latin American society—in labor relations, education, the treatment of minorities, the approach to diversity—to be a central problem in the transitions of the region. See his "Notes for the Study of Democratic Consolidation in Contemporary Latin America" (unpublished paper, Kellogg Institute, Notre Dame University, December 1985).

CHAPTER VI.

1. Thus, a constitutional charter adopted by a less than composite majority may not be a good measure of agreement. In general, if the test of agreement is the disappearance of breakdown games, the matter of how to verify it—by what indicator or measure—becomes difficult. I treat such measurement problems at greater length in "Parliaments, Consolidation, Institutionalization: A Minimalist View," in *Parliament and Democratic Consolidation in Southern Europe*, ed. Ulrike Liebert and Maurizio Cotta (London: Pinter, 1990).

2. Albert O. Hirschman, *A Bias for Hope* (New Haven: Yale University Press, 1971), pp. 323–26.

3. Hirschman himself (ibid., pp. 31–33) remarks that the development of consonant attitudes may not always follow behavior, that cognitive dissonance theory may excessively deny human choice and freedom, and that human action has unintended consequences that may cause actors to break out of a path.

4. I am reminded here of Hirschman's distinction between voice and exit as quite different ways of responding to a deficit of collective goals. See his *Exit, Voice, and Loyalties* (Cambridge: Harvard University Press, 1970).

5. In a formal theoretical analysis of decisional rules in democratic institutions, Douglas Rae shows that institutions that are more democratic do not necessarily produce greater satisfaction with individual decisions. See Douglas Rae, "Political Democracy as a Property of Political Institutions," *American Political Science Review* 65 (March 1971): 111–29.

6. Also, Spain and Italy are actually less than satisfactory examples. What I am discussing is democratic life following co-optative agreements that seek above all to remove breakdown games.

The Spanish agreement was defective on this score to begin with. Even so, Juan Linz argues that only late in the life of the Spanish republic was the point of no return reached; see his "From Great Hopes to Civil War: The Breakdown of Democracy in Spain," in *The Breakdown of Democratic Regimes: Europe* ed. Juan Linz and Alfred Stepan (Baltimore: Johns Hopkins University Press, 1978). As to Italy, the more interesting point is that the agreement had not even been formed; hence the collapse of democratic hopes. This leaves the Weimar Republic, if even that, as a more appropriate example; though the fact that breakdown games were revived in earnest more than a decade after the founding of the republic, the fact that the rise of the Nazi party was also a late, sudden development, and the presence of other intervening domestic and international developments all raise questions about whether the brunt of the explanation for democratic collapse can be placed on "birth defects" and on the inherent inadequacies of the democratic game.

7. These points are amply analyzed in Guillermo O'Donnell, "Notes for the Study of Democratic Consolidation in Latin America" (unpublished paper, Kellogg Institute, Notre Dame University, December 1985). It should be further noted that, even in the presence of civilian prodding, the military may not wish to act against a democratic government. Despite a political climate that stimulated military resentment (postwar demobilization, a less than satisfactory peace treaty, continuous taunting of the army by the left), civilian prodding of the Italian army during the crisis that led to fascism had limited effects, especially at the higher echelons of the institution.

8. Peter McDonough, Samuel H. Barnes, and Antonio López Pina, "The Growth of Democratic Legitimacy in Spain," *American Political Science Review* 80 (September 1986): 735–60. This and other papers by the same authors reveal how complex and fluid are the criteria of legitimacy that people employ. They also reveal, in keeping with a larger literature, that the objects of political support are various and not so simply related.

9. Hence the use of pacts can equally be dismissed when com-

prehensive reformers, insensitive to the risks of discounting their adversaries, control the transition.

10. As implied in the last chapter, some yet unclear combination of the latter two seems to be missing in most of the present Latin American transitions. The combination is absent in part because of the pressure of socioeconomic emergencies, and in part because the animosity and discredit that have accompanied the crisis of the dictatorships make it difficult to enter into explicit pacts with their representatives.

11. See, for instance, McDonough, Barnes, and López Pina, "Growth of Democratic Legitimacy."

12. This limitation still left many reforms for the democratic governments to engage in. They touch on civil liberties, education, family and gender legislation, and so forth. In general, reforms of this type, aided by a growing popular sensitivity, hold great importance for removing a culture of traditionalism and authoritarianism at the micro level. They are much more accepted today than they were, even in European democracies, in the postwar period or between the two wars. At the same time, unless the reforms are introduced with a vindictive Jacobin spirit reminiscent of the 1930s, they do not seem of a type to rally the insurmountable opposition of injured corporate interests.

13. See n. 24, chap. 4.

14. Japan and Italy have not yet achieved government turnover. This does not mean, however, that the two democracies suffer from a problem of legitimacy.

15. Q. Your party is called socialist. What does that mean to you? (*Time,* October 23, 1989)

A. Ask the Hungarians to help me on this one. (Felipe Gonzáles)

16. The proviso raises questions of whether this statement, and the illustrations that follow, can be extended to areas such as Latin America where the very ability to reach a democratic agreement seems to require pacts—yet pacts have recently eluded the region. I shall return to the point.

17. So, at least, I wrote in "Founding Coalitions in Southern

Europe: Legitimacy and Hegemony," *Government and Opposition* 15 (Spring 1980): 162–89.

18. To understand the attitude of the left, it is important to keep in mind that, while pursuing a go-it-alone strategy, the transitional government, as a move toward full political democratization, also repealed postwar legislation that restricted the organization of "suspect" political movements. On this and other aspects of the Greek transition, see Nikiforos Diamandouros, "Transition to, and Consolidation of, Democratic Politics in Greece, 1974–1983: A Tentative Assessment," *Western European Politics* 7 (April 1987): 50–71.

19. In this case, political actors will in all likelihood show special forbearance in the period of institutional implementation, just as they demonstrate tolerance toward the openness of the democratic game and the uncertainty of its outcomes. In fact, when all political actors share a democratic bias, they may well be satisfied with a sketchy agreement, detailing only the broad parameters of the democratic game. Hence, the implementation of the agreement may safely accommodate alternative institutional and procedural solutions.

20. For the distinction between majoritarian (or Westminster) and consensus democracy see Arend Lijphart, *Democracies: Patterns of Majoritarian and Consensus Government in Twenty-One Countries* (New Haven: Yale University Press, 1984).

21. Yet for all the complaints about the imperfections of some constitutional charters, resistance to altering their delicate balance by legislation is, revealingly, almost the rule. When muddling through does not suffice, judicial review is a more legitimate way of settling contrasting interpretations.

22. Giuseppe Di Palma, "The European and the Central American Experience," in *The Central American Impasse,* ed. Giuseppe Di Palma and Laurence Whitehead (London: Croom Helm, 1986).

CHAPTER VII.

1. Samuel P. Huntington, *Political Order in Changing Societies* (New Haven: Yale University Press, 1968), p. 12.

2. Criteria and measures of consolidation are discussed in

Guillermo O'Donnell, "Notes on the Study of Democratic Consolidation in Contemporary Latin America" (unpublished paper, Kellogg Institute, Notre Dame University, December 1985), and in Giuseppe Di Palma, "Parliaments, Consolidation, Institutionalization: A Minimalist View," in *Parliament and Democratic Consolidation in Southern Europe,* ed. Ulrike Liebert and Maurizio Cotta (London: Pinter, 1990).

3. See chap. 6, n. 2.

4. Guillermo O'Donnell, "Notes on the Study of Democratic Consolidation," p. 19.

5. A softer variant of this position is that deep-seated political orientations cannot be captured reliably by public opinion research. It is difficult to assess from a questionnaire or interview how permanent or transient a declared political belief may be.

6. See chap. 5, n. 8. The importance of time in the development of certain aspects of a democratic political culture is empirically analyzed in Philip Converse's classic work: "Of Time and Partisan Stability," *Comparative Political Studies* 2 (July 1969): 139–71.

7. See chap. 3, nn. 9 and 12.

8. See chap. 6, n. 7.

9. See chap. 2, n. 16.

10. We should not be misled by the ability of authoritarian movements to rally imposing crowds to commemorate dead dictators and historical events of the past regime. Symbolic attendance, the comradely return to a mythical and mystical past, the resurrection of rituals and paraphernalia, may have psychological more than political significance. Thus, I wonder how many of those who attend such communal affairs vote for the masters of ceremony.

11. For an interesting historical and cultural analysis of the reasons why, on the other hand, these developments in public opinion may still not amount to the formation of a democratic political culture, see Mihály Vajda, "East-Central European Perspectives," in *Civil Society and the State: New European Perspectives,* ed. John Keane (London and New York: Verso, 1988). Vajda also distinguishes between Eastern and east-central Europe. For a

more discursive analysis that focuses more directly on the present diffusion of Western life-style models, see Orville Schell, *Discos and Democracy: China in the Throes of Reform* (New York: Pantheon, 1988).

12. Quoted anonymously in the *New York Review of Books,* June 15, 1989. Not knowing how to relinquish, in fact how to limit, power is not a promising predicament. China after Tiananmen Square is the most recent and dramatic case in point, but it is not the only one. If authoritarian elites do not know how to relinquish or limit their power, democrats might step in (the Philippines in 1986, Italy in 1943). But the dictatorship may just as well reassert itself (Poland in 1981). It is also true that there may be no better teacher of how to relinquish power than the growing realization that the time to relinquish it has come.

13. An interesting comparative analysis of the subjective vs. objective causes of poor performance and democratic breakdown is contained in the first chapter of Franklin H. Adler, "Italian Industrialists from Liberalism to Fascism" (Ph.D. diss., University of Chicago, 1980).

14. The evidence on whether democracy promotes economic growth more than dictatorship is inconclusive when the question is addressed so broadly. Again, the important point is perceptions. Even though expectations about democracy may have decreased, the question is whether they are now higher than expectations about dictatorship. For contrasting findings about economic growth and regime type, see Adam Przeworski, "Party Systems and Economic Development" (Ph.D. diss., Northwestern University, 1966); William Dick, "Authoritarian versus Nonauthoritarian Approaches to Economic Development," *Journal of Political Economy* 82 (1974): 817–27; and Samuel Huntington and Jorge Dominguez, "Political Development," in *Handbook of Political Science,* ed. Fred I. Greenstein and Nelson W. Polsby, vol. 3, *Macropolitical Theory* (Reading: Addison-Wesley, 1975). See also chap. 2, n. 2.

15. If economic reforms require sacrifices, then sacrifices without political gains are self-defeating. If reforms involve economic liberalization that benefit at least some producers and consumers, then economic liberalization may spill over, and may have to spill

over, onto political demands. *Perestroika* without *glasnost* is a bit like squaring the circle. The ultimate and already raised question—can Communist political classes afford and enact economic liberalization and a return to the market?—is still to be addressed.

16. More precisely, the relation between material performance and support may not be monotonic. Support may suddenly drop only when performance gets to be abysmally low, causing drastic cuts in already low popular consumption, or the maintenance of consumption at drastic costs to capital reproduction, or both. In these cases intervening factors of the type discussed in the text may offer little or no help.

17. The fact that citizens may attribute every aspect of collective performance to the government is a finding. The fact that analysts may do likewise is unfortunate. Yet analysts often employ aggregate statistics—rates of inflation or unemployment, balances of payments, budgetary outlays and deficits, gross national product, money supplies, rates of investment, prime rates—as quick indicators of how governments are doing. When such aggregates are applied to new democracies, we often discover, not surprisingly, that their governments perform poorly. Yet economic aggregates are only what policy analysts call outcomes, and outcomes have no clear connection with policies intentionally instituted by governments. Although policies have consequences that deserve study, starting from outcomes begs the question. See for a critical analysis centered on these points, Thomas John Bossert, "Can We Return to the Regime for Comparative Policy Analysis? or, the State and Health Policies in Central America," *Comparative Politics* 15 (July 1983): 419–41.

18. Convincing empirical evidence, focusing on Spain, on this and other following points is found in Peter McDonough, Samuel H. Barnes, and Antonio López Pina, "Economic Policy and Public Opinion in Spain," *American Journal of Political Science* 30 (May 1986): 446–79.

19. On the self-serving nature of liberalization, in contrast to democratization, Aleksandr Gelman, a member of the Soviet cinematographers' organization, writes colorfully: "Democratization provides for the redistribution of power, rights, and free-

doms, the creation of a number of independent structures of management and information. And liberalization is the conservation of all the foundations of the administrative system but in a milder form. Liberalization is an unclenched fist, but the hand is the same and at any moment it could be clenched again into a fist. Only outwardly is liberalization sometimes reminiscent of democratization, but in actual fact it is a fundamental and intolerable usurpation." (Cited in Zbigniew Brzezinski, *The Grand Failure* [New York: Scribner's, 1989], pp. 45–46.)

20. Of course, the capacity of each *dictablanda* to endure can differ substantially from case to case. A variation on the theme of endurance is the fact that in Argentina, always a difficult case for me to pigeonhole, the military skipped the *dictablanda* stage and relinquished power before finding a solution for its new institutional role; yet, because of this, the military still escapes the control of the competitive system. But these differences in the capacity to resist the democratic option are more appropriately dealt with in the next chapter.

CHAPTER VIII.

1. Samuel P. Huntington, "Will More Countries Become Democratic?" *Political Science Quarterly* 99 (Summer 1984): 193–218.

2. Zbigniew Brzezinski, *The Grand Failure* (New York: Scribner's, 1989), pp. 135–36. Brzezinski's broad statement is subjected to considerable qualifications, however, as his analysis proceeds.

3. Huntington, "Will More Countries Become Democratic?" p. 217.

4. Beginning in the 1960s, a vast revisionist literature has appeared, reassessing the concept of totalitarianism, its application to Soviet and East European communism, and Communist political evolution. My simple reference to a totalitarian/post-totalitarian dichotomy does not do justice to the richness and diversity of the literature. Still, there is little if anything in that literature that conceptually anticipates today's changes. An excellent review of the revisionist literature and classification of its theoretical strands

is Andrew Janos, *Politics and Paradigms: Changing Theories of Change in Social Science* (Stanford: Stanford University Press, 1986), chap. 4.

5. Jeane Kirkpatrick, "Dictatorships and Double Standards," *Commentary* 68 (November 1979): 34–46.

6. Among the few exceptions, we may want to include the newly industrializing countries of East Asia. There, the incentive to democratize originating in their economic progress may be offset (despite the countries' lesser problem in dealing with social inequalities and conservatism while democratizing) by the fact that their economic progress is singularly, though not necessarily, associated with their regimes. So why democratize? But even among these countries, there exist some (South Korea, Taiwan) whose greater international visibility and ambitions, whose role as models against their Communist counterparts, and whose greater politicization may weigh more heavily—both in creating resentment against the regimes and in inducing the regimes to seek reform. This means that international factors, with which I will close the essay, also enter into the democratic calculus.

7. Kenneth Jowitt uses the concept of neotraditionalism to describe the evolution of communism under Brezhnev. The interpretation is shared by other authors, and so is the interpretation of post-totalitarian trends as leading some Communist regimes toward military rule infused with nationalism, chauvinism, and praetorianism. Whatever concept or category we use, the argument I am developing stays largely intact. Accordingly, the regimes we are describing should have very few reasons to accept being dislodged. See Kenneth Jowitt, "Soviet Neotraditionalism: The Political Corruption of a Leninist Regime," *Soviet Studies* 35 (July 1983): 275–97.

8. A more detailed analysis of the points that follow in the text is found in my "European and the Central American Experience," in *The Central American Impasse,* ed. Giuseppe Di Palma and Laurence Whitehead (London: Croom Helm, 1986).

9. Even in the case of Spain, where the army both installed and temporarily ran the dictatorship, the new regime emphasized de-

politicization and demobilization, and the state apparatus still presented itself as the historically impartial guarantor of a reconstituted legal order.

10. See chap. 5, n. 16.

11. For a recent statement on Central American dictatorships, see Enrique Baloyra-Herp, "Reactionary Despotism in Central America," *Journal of Latin American Studies* 15 (1983): 295–319. For the military component of parasitic Central American regimes, see Alain Rouquié, *The Military and the State in Latin America* (Berkeley and Los Angeles: University of California Press, 1987), chap. 6.

12. Interview published in the Italian daily *La Repubblica,* August 25, 1989. Emphasis added.

13. Dankwart Rustow, "Transitions to Democracy," *Comparative Politics* 2 (April 1970): 337–63.

14. There may be, on the other hand, less overstatement in the model of Central American despotism. In its case, vulnerability to a stalemate, when it finally sets in, may reflect the very fact that those who unscrupulously run these regimes with predatory intents may not be insensitive, when everything else fails, to a drastic fall in material rewards.

15. For criticisms, along these lines, of model-building in Communist studies, see Jerry F. Hough, *The Soviet Union and Social Science Theory* (Cambridge: Harvard University Press, 1977), chap. 11.

16. The point is eloquently made in Enrique A. Baloyra, "Democratic Transition in Comparative Perspective," in *Comparing New Democracies,* ed. Enrique A. Baloyra (Boulder: Westview Press, 1987), pp. 44–47.

17. On the uses of elections in El Salvador, see Terry Karl, "Democracy by Design: The Christian Democratic Party in El Salvador," in *The Central American Impasse,* ed. Di Palma and Whitehead.

18. Nicaragua, not a despotic regime in the sense I have given the term, is included in the proposed settlement. A separate analysis of the Sandinista regime is not part of my task. In its place, it is worth pointing out the importance of the electoral pact that,

within the regional settlement, the Sandinista government and the opposition parties have signed in the summer of 1989, for the purpose, also, of defusing armed violence.

19. See for example the treatment of El Salvador in the 1970s and early 1980s, in Enrique A. Baloyra, *El Salvador in Transition* (Chapel Hill: University of North Carolina Press, 1982). See also Piero Gleijeses, "The Case for Power Sharing in El Salvador," *Foreign Affairs* 61 (Summer 1983): 1048–63.

20. The importance of international referents and the way they have changed are underscored in Andrew Janos, "Social Theory and the Dynamics of Political Change in Communist Societies" (working paper, University of California, Berkeley, August 1989). Janos derives from the changes implications for Communist transformations more guarded than mine, and with different emphases.

21. Ibid., p. 16.

22. The best example is the repression of the Prague Spring, for attempting more than tactical domestic and global shifts.

23. The fall of Khrushchev can be understood in this light as the price for threatening, by the personalistic improvisations of his reforms, the status and influence of Soviet *nomenklaturas* at a time when their status and influence were at their functional peak.

24. On the social contract and its limits, see chap. 5, n. 19.

25. In China after Mao, problems with the internal cohesiveness of the political class, and with its loyalty to the leadership, have time and again been tackled by using one sector of the class to hammer others into submission. But the resulting pendulum of reforms followed by retrenchment exposes the unresolved problem of leadership succession and, underneath it, a persistent conflict within the political class and its leadership. China's toying with a market economy within autocratic government evokes the political model of the newly industrializing countries of Asia. But unless China can replicate the successes of the latter, the cohesiveness and endurance of its political class may be more appropriately compared to that of the less successful examples of bureaucratic authoritarianism—the examples of Latin America.

26. Why economic reforms should be easier in China is discussed in Brzezinski, *Grand Failure*, pt. 4, esp. chap. 16. Why

China is more hesitant about politico-institutional reforms that affect the unity of its political class, and is resisting the spillage of economic reforms onto political ones, is another matter.

27. In Hungary support for a reformed party appeared, by all opinion polls, to hover in mid-1989 around 25 percent; in Poland, that support at the inauguration of the first non-Communist government appeared almost nonexistent.

28. By comparison, the single parties of right-wing dictatorships have less interest in their own reformed survival. In a democracy, these parties typically languish and their cadres are dispersed—revealing the exceptional nature of the dictatorships that produced them and the fact that the parties were contingent coalitions of disparate interests, less rooted in any popular groups and in the mass-based political and partisan traditions of their own countries.

29. Adjusting to a multiparty system did, and will, require a different understanding not only of a Communist party's external role but also of its internal organization and relations. The latter is especially delicate because it affects the ability of a reformed party to keep different functional components of the old party together under a new organization, more suited for competitive politics. But, judging at least from the interview reported earlier in the chapter, there is a surprisingly clear understanding among some Communist cadres of what this must entail. Answering a question in that interview (see n. 12) about future relations between his parliamentary group and the party's central committee, the leader of the Communist group in the Polish lower house comments as follows: "We do not want to impose ourselves upon the central committee, but we wish to be a pulling force, not just executors. As among Western parties, our members of parliament must be better represented in the central committee and the political bureau. A fusion between central committee and parliamentary group is not ruled out."

30. Jerry F. Hough, *Russia and the West: Gorbachev and the Politics of Reform* (New York: Simon and Schuster, 1988).

31. If abandoned by the party, the only force capable of breakdown games would be the military. But, provided domestic tran-

quillity and prudence in dealing with Communist bloc relations are sought—which seems to be the case in the scenario of reforms I am presenting here—it would seem that in Eastern Europe the military should have less interest in stepping in than it had in many or most right-wing dictatorships of clear military origin. We should also consider that "Bonapartism" has never sat well with European Communist regimes. Part of their founding myth is that the party speaks heroically for the nation and that, more than other institutions, the military is subordinate to the party and integrated within the regime. Thus, it is one thing for Communist leaders to recognize the military as one institution bolstering with other institutions a process of reforms guided by the party; it is another to accept that it preempt the party. The case of Poland, where an army general and head of the state offers himself as guarantor of a dialogue, is exemplary in this regard.

CHAPTER IX.

1. A more difficult variation on removing vetoes, of equal relevance to the Soviet case, is the lifting of a veto against the political autonomy of nationalities within a multinational state, favoring in turn radical changes in their political systems.

2. See chap. 8, n. 6.

3. In a much publicized article, Francis Fukuyama has recently announced the possible emergence of Western liberal democracy as the final form of human government. See Fukuyama, "The End of History?" *National Interest* 16 (Summer 1989): 3–18.

4. The Italian case, as I have already argued, should not be likened to that of the other two defeated dictatorships.

5. Instead, the occupying forces placed emphasis, especially in Japan, on the need to democratize society and the old state institutions—to avoid, by a combination of legal reforms, mass education and resocialization, a return to the past.

6. These lines were written well before American removal of the Noriega regime in Panama. The argument still stands.

7. Laurence Whitehead, "International Aspects of Democratization," in *Transitions from Authoritarian Rule: Comparative Perspectives,* ed. Guillermo O'Donnell, Philippe C. Schmitter, and

Laurence Whitehead (Baltimore: Johns Hopkins University Press), esp. pp. 10–19.

8. Ibid., pp. 17–18.

9. For a comparative analysis and data on the importance of external support in building and maintaining domestic violence (in particular, insurgency) see Karl Jackson, "Post-Colonial Rebellion and Counter-Insurgency," in *Armed Communist and Separatist Movements in Southeast Asia,* ed. Chandram Jeshuran (Singapore: Institute of Southeast Asia Studies, 1986).

10. The vital importance of international factors in Central America does not diminish the ultimate role that domestic factors play, both in explaining and in treating the plight.

11. My colleague George Breslauer suggests in a personal communication that "the American posture in Central America [is] closer to the Khrushchevian or Brezhnevite (more the former) posture toward Eastern Europe. Earlier Soviet leaders, while willing to encourage East European emulation of the partial, post-totalitarian reforms going on in their countries, were more preoccupied with "anti-imperialism" in that region. . . . Analogously, while the U.S. is willing to push for democratization of sorts in Central America, the price it is willing to pay toward that end is bounded sharply by a larger preoccupation with 'anticommunism' in the region."

12. Again, the remarks date a few weeks before the opening of the Berlin Wall on November 9, 1989.

13. Because Romania has discarded that fiction long ago, under international and domestic conditions that did not threaten the national dictatorship, the crisis of hegemony in the rest of Eastern Europe does not touch its leadership. Notice also how Ceausescu has moved closer to the patrimonial and predatory despotism of Central America. Thus, open repression/open conflict are more likely.

14. In part, a lesser attention to the hegemonic dimension leads other authors to different assessments of Chinese vs. Soviet reform prospects. See Zbigniew Brzezinski, *The Grand Failure* (New York: Scribner's, 1989), chap. 4; and Constance Squires Meaney, "Is the

Soviet Present China's Future?" *World Politics* 39 (January 1987): 203–30.

15. Even if the Soviet Union possessed the economic capabilities to retool itself as a trader in an internationalized economy—which it does not—it would never settle for such a role.

16. Cited in Louis Althusser, *For Marx* (London: Penguin Books, 1969), p. 120.

Index

Africa: democratization in, 2, 164
After the Revolution? (Dahl), 42
Aquino, Corazon, 84
Argentina, 155
Asia: democratization in, 2, 48, 164, 186
Austria: democratization of, 32
Authoritarianism: compared with totalitarianism, 35, 158; and democratization from within, 36–39, 48–49, 77, 78–79, 148; internal failure of, 37–38; Left and, 68–70; nature of, 33, 35–36, 147, 160–61; self-initiated reform of, 62–65

Barnes, Samuel, 119, 146
Bolivia, 104
Bourgeoisie, economic: and democratization, 77, 90–94, 95–97, 100; and economic pacts, 93; in Latin America, 92
Brazil: elections in, 82, 83; regime transition in, 103, 155

"Breakdown games," 110–11, 112, 114, 118, 120, 127, 134, 145, 162, 185
Brezhnev, Leonid, 173
Brzezinski, Zbigniew: on democratic transitions, 157–58

Center (political): and democratization, 56–57; as moderating influence between Right and Left, 50–53, 54–55, 56–57, 70
Central America: democratization in, 12, 81, 165–70, 181, 194; international pacts in, 167, 192; military authoritarianism in, 159, 160–62, 165–66, 167–69, 170–71; negotiated settlements in, 167–68. *See also* Latin America
Cerezo, Vinicio, 155
Chile: referendum in, 85, 154
China, 21, 36, 159, 164, 172, 173, 175, 193; hegemony of, 197–98

Text and Display: Sabon
Compositor: Maple-Vail Book Manufacturing Group
Printer and Binder: Maple-Vail Book Manufacturing Group